redefining
life: MYCAREER

A NAVSTUDY FEATURING THE**MESSAGE**®//REMIX™

Written and compiled by Margaret Feinberg

TH1NK
P.O. Box 35001
Colorado Springs, Colorado 80935

www.navpress.com

TH1NK is an imprint of NavPress.

TH1NK and the TH1NK logo are registered trademarks of NavPress. Absence of ® in connection with marks of NavPress or other parties does not indicate an absence of registration of those marks.

ISBN 1-57683-887-0

Cover design by Kirk DouPonce, DogEaredDesign.com
Cover photo by Shannon Fagan, Getty
Creative Team: Nicci Jordan, Steve Parolini, Arvid Wallen, Kathy Mosier, Bob Bubnis

Written and compiled by Margaret Feinberg

All Scripture quotations in this publication are taken from *THE MESSAGE* (MSG). Copyright © 1993, 1994, 1995, 1996, 2000, 2001, 2002. Used by permission of NavPress Publishing Group.

Printed in the United States of America

1 2 3 4 5 6 7 8 9 10 / 09 08 07 06 05

FOR A FREE CATALOG OF
NAVPRESS BOOKS & BIBLE STUDIES,
CALL 1-800-366-7788 (USA)
OR 1-800-839-4769 (CANADA)

contents

about the redefininglife series

It's in Christ that we find out who we are and what we are living for.

Ephesians 1:11

For most of your life, you've been a student. And yet in a moment—probably marked by a ceremony—the title you carried for more than a dozen years was stripped away. So now how will you describe yourself when people ask? Are you a professional? An adult? A temporarily unemployed graduate? What seems to fit? Or do any of these fit at all?

Expectations are probably pretty high. But only a few of your graduating class fall into the life you wish you could have—the great job, the wonderful lifelong relationship, the incredible devotion to God. For the rest of you, it's back to square one in many ways. What has been defined for you in the past is suddenly up for negotiation.

The discussion guides in the REDEFINING LIFE series give you a forum to help with that negotiation process. They can help you figure out who you are, *who you really are,* whether you're still taking classes, employed full-time, or somewhere in between. They can help you find out what's really important in life, how to thrive in your work, and how to grow lifelong, meaningful relationships.

REDEFINING LIFE is a place to ask the hard questions of yourself and others. We're talking about a "marrow deep" kind of honesty. At the very least, these discussion guides will show you that you're not alone in the process of self-definition. And hopefully, they will also give you a glimpse—or maybe more—of God's role in the defining of you.

introduction

God spoke: "Let us make human beings in our image,
make them reflecting our nature So they can be
responsible for the fish in the sea, the birds in
the air, the cattle, And, yes, Earth itself, and
every animal that moves on the face of Earth."
God created human beings; he created them godlike,
Reflecting God's nature. He created them male and
female. God blessed them: "Prosper! Reproduce!
Fill Earth! Take charge! Be responsible for fish
in the sea and birds in the air, for every living
thing that moves on the face of Earth."

Genesis 1:26-28

Since the beginning, work was part of God's design for people. It wasn't until after the fall of mankind when the penalty of sin kicked in that work became hard and at times even "painful" (Genesis 3:17). Even today, work is often a blend of pleasure and pain. It can be a source of tremendous satisfaction and joy but also one of difficulty. Maybe that's one reason figuring out a career or your life's work is so challenging. We want the joy without the hardship. We want to do what God designed without any of the disappointment that comes from living in a fallen world.

In this discussion guide you are going to examine your work life and attempt to discover ways to grow in your job or your career. Maybe you haven't found the "right job" yet—maybe you haven't found *any* job yet. Whatever your circumstance, it's important to evaluate your workplace life because that's where you'll be spending most of your waking hours in the years to come. That fact might seem a bit disheartening if you're not enjoying your work today, but with the guidance of Scripture and the wisdom of those who have gone before, you *can* find fulfillment in your career.

Take the time to evaluate your workplace life—think about what you want from work and the challenges you face. Then explore these issues in depth as you go through this discussion guide on your own and with your small group.

how to
use this
discussion guide

REDEFINING LIFE isn't like any other study. We're not kidding. REDEFINING LIFE isn't designed with easy, obvious-to-answer questions and nice fill-in-the-blanks. It's got more of a wide-open-spaces feel to it.

The process is simple, really. Complete a lesson *on your own* (see details below). Then get with your small group and go through it again *together*. Got it?

Okay, want a little more direction than that? Here you go. And if you want even more help, check out the Discussion Group Study Tips (page 135) and the Frequently Asked Questions (page 137) sections in the back of the book.

1. Read, read, read. Each lesson contains five sections, but don't think of them as homework. This isn't an assignment to be graded. And at the end of the week, you don't have to turn it in to a teacher, professor, or boss. So don't read this as a "have to" but as a "get to." Think about how you read when you're on vacation. Set a leisurely pace. Try to enjoy what you read. Then read it again. Allow the words and

first thoughts
like:
dislike:
agree:
disagree:
don't get it:

meaning to soak in. Use the First Thoughts box to record your initial reactions to the text. (That's a sample on the previous page.) Then use the space provided in and around the reading to make notes. What bugs you? What inspires you? What doesn't make sense? What's confusing? Be honest. Be real. Be yourself. Don't shy away from phrases or sentences you don't understand or don't like. Circle them. Cross them out. Add exclamation marks or smiley faces.

2. Think about what you read. Think about what you wrote. Always ask:

- What does this mean?
- Why does this matter?
- How does this relate to my life right now?
- What does Scripture have to say about this?

Then respond to the questions provided. If you have a knack for asking questions, don't be shy about writing some of your own. You may have a lot to say on one topic, little on another. That's okay. When you come back to the passages in your small group, listen. Allow the experience of others to broaden your understanding and wisdom. You'll be stretched here—called on to evaluate what you've discovered and asked to make practical sense of it. In community, that stretching can often be painful and sometimes even embarrassing. But your willingness to be transparent—your openness to the possibility of personal growth—will reap great rewards. Vulnerability spurs growth in yourself and others.

3. Pray as you go through the entire session—before you begin reading, as you're thinking about a passage and its questions, and especially before you get together in a small group. Pause 'n' pray whenever you need to ask God for help along the way. Prayer takes many forms. You can speak your prayers. Be silent. Write them in the space at the bottom of each page. You can pray a Scripture or a spiritual song. Just don't forget that one of the most important parts of prayer is taking time to listen for God's response.

4. Live. What good are study, reflection, and prayer if they don't lead to action? When reflecting on the week's worth of lessons, think about what impacted you and how you can turn that lesson into action. After studying the issue of forgiveness, you may realize you need to write a letter or email to someone. After studying God's generosity, you may feel compelled to give a gift to a particular outreach. Figure out what God is calling you to do to live out your faith. Sometimes you'll finish a week's worth of lessons and each group member will decide to commit to the same goal. Other times you'll each walk away with a different conviction or goal. Record your goals in the book.

5. Follow up. What good are information and conversation if they don't lead to transformation? Your goal in doing any good study is to ultimately become more like Christ, and this is no exception. Prepare yourself to take your faith and make it active and alive. Be willing to set goals and hold others (as well as be held) accountable in your group. Part of being in a community of Jesus-followers means asking, "Hey, did you do what you said you were going to do?" It will help you put your faith into action as part of a community.

6. Repeat as necessary.

uncovering
gifts
and talents

And that special gift of ministry you were given when the leaders of the church laid hands on you and prayed—keep that dusted off and in use.

1 Timothy 4:14

the defining line

We start every lesson by asking you to do a sometimes-difficult thing: define the core truths about the study topic as it relates to you right now. Use this "beginning place" to set the foundation for the lesson. You can then build, change, adjust, and otherwise redefine your life from here.

You are a one-of-a-kind handiwork of God. You are a unique blend of talents, gifts, strengths, weaknesses, likes, and dislikes. No one is quite like you. And no one can contribute in quite the same way.

If you're going to effectively use your natural gifts and talents in the workplace, you need to know what they are. You need to know what you're good at and not so good at. In the space below make a list of ten things you're good at.

Now make a list of five things you're not so good at.

Of the activities you do most often, how many come from the first list? How many come from the second? Why? Are there any activities on your first list that you haven't done in a while? What prevents you from doing them more often?

How much time and energy do you spend in a typical week developing your talents and gifts? Are you intentional about using them? Why or why not? What could you do to be more intentional?

Consider sharing your responses with your group when you meet.

read Entrusted

1 Kings 3:5-14

That night, there in Gibeon, GOD appeared to Solomon in a dream: God said, "What can I give you? Ask."

Solomon said, "You were extravagantly generous in love with David my father, and he lived faithfully in your presence, his relationships were just and his heart right. And you have persisted in this great and generous love by giving him—and this very day!—a son to sit on his throne.

"And now here I am: GOD, my God, you have made me, your servant, ruler of the kingdom in place of David my father. I'm too young for this, a mere child! I don't know the ropes, hardly know the 'ins' and 'outs' of this job. And here I am, set down in the middle of the people you've chosen, a great people—far too many to ever count.

"Here's what I want: Give me a God-listening heart so I can lead your people well, discerning the difference between good and evil. For who on their own is capable of leading your glorious people?"

God, the Master, was delighted with Solomon's response. And God said to him, "Because you have asked for this and haven't grasped after a long life, or riches, or the doom of your enemies, but you have asked for the ability to lead and govern well, I'll give you what you've asked for—I'm giving you a wise and mature heart. There's never been one like you before; and there'll be no one after. As a bonus, I'm giving you both the wealth and glory you didn't ask for—there's not a king anywhere who will come up to your mark. And if you stay on course, keeping your

first thoughts

like:

dislike:

agree:

disagree:

don't get it:

eye on the life-map and the God-signs as your father David did, I'll also give you a long life."

think

- If you could ask God for one gift—other than the wisdom Solomon requested—what would you ask for? Why?
- What has stopped you from asking God for this one thing?
- Where do all gifts come from? Why do you think it's so easy to forget the source of your talents and gifts? In what situations are you most tempted to forget that your talents are a gift?
- Why do you think people are given different gifts? How many gifts do you think the average person is given? How many gifts do you think the average person actually develops and uses?
- What keeps people from using more of their gifts?
- What is the appropriate response to the gifts you've been given?

pray

read What Are You Naturally Good At? (Part One)

From *Welcome to the Real World: You've Got an Education—Now Get a Life!* by
Stacy Kravetz[1]

Use the following skill areas to remind yourself of things you can do.

1. Create. Not just the ability to draw or paint, but an eye for arranging objects, combining colors, visualizing new ways to present old things. Do you walk into a room and immediately see ways to arrange the furniture better? Do you come up with slogans for products and wonder why no one else has thought of them? Have you played in a band or written short stories for fun, but never considered how your talents might translate into a career?

2. Analyze. You could be sitting around with friends who are debating an issue in the news and realize you could make a case for either side. Your skill might be seeing all the angles and using them to make a persuasive argument. When you think back on the courses you did well in, were they more like ones where you'd analyze literature or where you'd calculate statistics problem sets and come up with one answer?

3. Remember details. Some people are better at making associations and remembering broad concepts, while others have a better memory for names, dates, and other specifics. Neither is better in and of itself, but one might suit a certain career better than the other.

4. Deal with people. Some people have a natural rapport with strangers and can talk to anyone about anything. It's a great skill to have if you choose a career where you deal with people all day long, but there are all kinds of jobs that don't require this type of interaction. Do you like meeting and talking to new people? How do you feel about addressing a large group? Are you more comfortable one-on-one? Do you like to negotiate or argue your point in person or do you prefer to do it on paper?

5. Handle stressful situations. Do you work best under deadline pressure or do you accomplish better work when no one's breathing down your neck? All jobs involve some degree of stress, but while some people thrive in a high-pressure environment, it's not for everyone. Can you work with lots of noise? Do you get energy from other people who are meeting their own deadlines? Do you meet every deadline, no matter how much caffeine or how many sleepless nights it takes? Do you let stress get to you or can you leave it behind when you're away from the work?

---

first thoughts

like:

dislike:

agree:

disagree:

don't get it:

---

think

- Put a star by the skill areas that come naturally to you. Put an arrow by the skill areas that are more difficult for you. In what ways does your current job reflect your strengths? In what ways does it reflect your weaknesses?
- Which of the skill areas are your parents particularly good at? How do their strengths and weaknesses compare to yours?
- Why do you think it's important for people to know their strengths and weaknesses?
- What happens when people work outside of their skill areas? Have you ever worked outside of your skill areas? If so, what was the result?

pray

read What Are You Naturally Good At? (Part Two)

From *Welcome to the Real World: You've Got an Education—Now Get a Life!* by Stacy Kravetz[2]

6. Teach or explain. You may have seen math tutoring as a way to pay for extras during college, but looking back, maybe you got a lot of satisfaction from teaching. Do you like to figure out ways to present information? Do you get frustrated when people don't understand what you're trying to explain? Can you think of more than one way to teach or explain things? Are you good at organizing material?

7. Supervise or manage. Think about how you are among your friends: Are you the one who often plans the fiesta night or gets everyone together for an event? Do people come to you often for advice or answers? Are you good at delegating responsibility rather than taking everything on yourself? Do you get stressed when everything rests on your head because you're in charge or do you like that sense of control?

8. Motivate. Does it take a crane to get you out of bed in the morning to go to class or do your work? Do you put things off until the last minute or can you make yourself do work without torturing yourself? Do you need external deadlines or can you set them yourself? Have you come up with entrepreneurial ideas that you want to try out? Have you done well on long projects where you didn't have daily deadlines, such as writing a thesis or running a semester-long lab experiment?

9. Communicate. This includes spoken and written communication. Do you dread writing anything from a business letter to a paper for school or do people come to you for help with their writing? Have you always found it easy to express yourself? Are you good at structuring and formulating ideas? Are you a good self-editor or a good editor of other people's work?

10. Brainstorm. Some people are building the better mousetrap, even outside the context of career. Have you started projects on your own as hobbies? Do you constantly come up with new ideas for products you wish existed? Are you good at coming up with ideas in a group brainstorming session?

---

first thoughts

like:

dislike:

agree:

disagree:

don't get it:

---

think

- Put a star by the skill areas that come naturally to you. Put an arrow by the skill areas that are more difficult for you. In what ways does your current job reflect your strengths? In what ways does it reflect your weaknesses?
- Which of the skill areas are your parents particularly good at? How do their strengths and weaknesses compare to yours?
- Now compare your responses in this section to those in the previous section. What are your top three strengths? What are your top three weaknesses? Are there any surprises among your responses? If so, explain.
- In what ways do your professional goals line up with your skill areas?

pray

read God's Gifts Handed Out

1 Corinthians 12:1-12

What I want to talk about now is the various ways God's Spirit gets worked into our lives. This is complex and often misunderstood, but I want you to be informed and knowledgeable. Remember how you were when you didn't know God, led from one phony god to another, never knowing what you were doing, just doing it because everybody else did it? It's different in this life. God wants us to use our intelligence, to seek to understand as well as we can. For instance, by using your heads, you know perfectly well that the Spirit of God would never prompt anyone to say "Jesus be damned!" Nor would anyone be inclined to say "Jesus is Master!" without the insight of the Holy Spirit.

God's various gifts are handed out everywhere; but they all originate in God's Spirit. God's various ministries are carried out everywhere; but they all originate in God's Spirit. God's various expressions of power are in action everywhere; but God himself is behind it all. Each person is given something to do that shows who God is: Everyone gets in on it, everyone benefits. All kinds of things are handed out by the Spirit, and to all kinds of people! The variety is wonderful:

- wise counsel
- clear understanding
- simple trust
- healing the sick
- miraculous acts
- proclamation
- distinguishing between spirits
- tongues
- interpretation of tongues.

---

first thoughts

like:

dislike:

agree:

disagree:

don't get it:

All these gifts have a common origin, but are handed out one by one by the one Spirit of God. He decides who gets what, and when.

You can easily enough see how this kind of thing works by looking no further than your own body. Your body has many parts—limbs, organs, cells—but no matter how many parts you can name, you're still one body. It's exactly the same with Christ.

think

- How do you respond to the statement, "Each person is given something to do that shows who God is"? In what ways is this statement true in your life?
- Why do you think God gives people such diverse gifts? Are there any gifts you're tempted to view as more or less valuable than others? Why?
- Are you ever frustrated by the gifts God has given you? Do you ever wish for different gifts? Why or why not?

pray

read Content in Yourself

From the sermon "The Pin Oak, the Pine, the Pear, and the Pansy" by Rev. Dr. B. Richard Dennis[3]

An ancient legend tells of a king who walked into his garden one day to find almost everything withered and dying. Speaking to a pin oak near the gate, he learned that it was sick of life because it was not tall and beautiful like the pine. The pine was upset, for it could not bear delicious fruit like the pear tree, while the pear tree complained that it did not have the lovely odor of the spruce; and so it went throughout the entire garden. Coming to a pansy, however, the king saw its bright face full of cheerfulness. "Well, little flower," said the monarch, "I'm glad to find at least one that is happy in this discouraging scene." "Your majesty, I know I'm of small account, but I decided you wanted a pansy when you planted me. If you had desired an oak or a pear tree, you would have put one in my place. Therefore I've determined to be the best flower I can be!"

God made each of us with certain gifts, skills, and temperaments. No two are alike. You are uniquely you. Yet each person is part of the human collage, a beautiful puzzle created by God. You are part of the grand human puzzle that makes up the body of Christ. Without your special gifts, the

---

first thoughts

like:

dislike:

agree:

disagree:

don't get it:

---

puzzle is incomplete. Occasionally, I see a slogan from years ago that encapsulates the truth. "Without 'U,' the word CHRCH is incomplete."

In the ancient legend only the pansy knew the truth. The monarch landscaped the garden so that the oak could be a mighty oak, the pine a towering pine, the pear tree a veritable buffet of delight, and the pansy a beaming flower.

Human tendency, however, takes God's wonderful gifts and ranks them so that some are more valued than others. In the church there are the *spotlight gifts*, gifts that are obvious and naturally draw a lot of attention. Preaching, teaching, singing, and all types of performance gifts are usually the ones that grab the spotlight. Then, there are the *servant gifts*. These are the less-public gifts, like the gift of administration or the gift of nurturing or the gift of discernment or the gift of hospitality. We tend to ignore or downplay the *servant gifts*. No one applauds a particularly well-run committee meeting. We are as guilty today of applauding some gifts over others as did the Christians of the early church.

think

- In what ways do you resonate with the story this pastor told? In what situations are you tempted to try to be someone other than who you are?
- Do your natural gifts tend to fall into the category of "spotlight gifts" or "servant gifts"? Which category would you prefer? Why?
- This article talks about how gifts and talents should be used in the local *church*. How can you apply what it says to the *workplace*?
- Is there a correlation between your gifts and talents and the work you do? Should there be?

pray

live   The Redefining

Take a few moments to skim through the notes you've made in these readings. What do they reveal about the ways you use your talents and gifts? Based on what you've read and discussed, is there anything you want to change?

What, if anything, is stopping you from making this change?

What can you do in the upcoming months to develop your talents and gifts? What do you want to say to God (or ask of Him) in regard to this?

Are there things about yourself that you just don't like? Describe them.

Are you ever tempted to run away from your weaknesses or lack of talent in a particular area? What steps can you take to see yourself as Christ sees you—even in that area?

Talk with a close friend about all of the above. Brainstorm together about what it might take to move toward God in this area of your life. Determine what this looks like in a practical sense and then list any measurable goals you want to shoot for here. Review these goals each week to see how you're doing.

your unique
personality

For who do you know that really knows *you*, knows your heart? And even if they did, is there anything they would discover in you that you could take credit for? Isn't everything you *have* and everything you *are* sheer gifts from God? So what's the point of all this comparing and competing?

1 Corinthians 4:7

a reminder

Before you dive into this study, spend a little time reviewing what you wrote in the previous lesson's Live section. How are you doing? Check with your small-group members and review your progress toward the specified goals. If necessary, adjust your goals and plans and then recommit to them.

the defining line

Did you know that psychologists have identified thousands of personality traits and dimensions that differentiate people from each other? The particular combination of traits you have—whether instilled in you from the beginning through your genes or adopted from your environment or upbringing—makes you unique. You are like no other. (You probably have a few friends who would agree.)

We'll look at just a few traits to get things going. Circle the five words that best describe you from the following list:

Introverted	Extroverted
Reserved	Outgoing
Steady	Easily Excitable
Laid-back	Focused
Relaxed	Motivated

How do you feel about the words you circled? Do you ever wish you could be described with the words you didn't circle? On a scale of one to ten, with ten being the most, how content are you with yourself?

Consider sharing your responses with your group when you meet.

read Personality Traits

From *48 Days to the Work You Love* by Dan Miller[1]

Common personality traits are grouped into four categories:
1. Dominance (Driver)—Lion—Eagle: Takes charge, likes power and authority, confident, very direct, bold, determined, competitive.
2. Influencing (Expressive)—Otter—Peacock: Good talkers, outgoing, fun-loving, impulsive, creative, energetic, optimistic, variety-seeking, promoter.
3. Steadiness (Amiable)—Golden Retriever—Dove: Loyal, good listener, calm, enjoys routine, sympathetic, patient, understanding, reliable, avoids conflict.
4. Compliance (Analytical)—Beaver—Owl: Loves detail, very logical, diplomatic, factual, deliberate, controlled, inquisitive, predictable, resistance to change.

first thoughts

like:

dislike:

agree:

disagree:

don't get it:

think

- Underline the words in each of the personality types that best describe you. Which one or two personality types best describe you?
- Which one or two personality types do you tend to gravitate toward in your friendships and working relationships? Which one or two do you tend to gravitate away from?
- Are you at all uncomfortable with your personality type? Are there any personality types you wish you were more like? Why or why not? What steps can you take to become more comfortable with your personality type and who you are?
- Which traits in your predominant personality type do you see as advantages or strengths? Which do you see as weaknesses? What can you do to maximize your strengths and minimize your weaknesses?

pray

read Two Personality Types

Luke 10:38-42

As they continued their travel, Jesus entered a village. A woman by the name of Martha welcomed him and made him feel quite at home. She had a sister, Mary, who sat before the Master, hanging on every word he said. But Martha was pulled away by all she had to do in the kitchen. Later, she stepped in, interrupting them. "Master, don't you care that my sister has abandoned the kitchen to me? Tell her to lend me a hand."

The Master said, "Martha, dear Martha, you're fussing far too much and getting yourself worked up over nothing. One thing only is essential, and Mary has chosen it—it's the main course, and won't be taken from her."

---

first thoughts

like:

dislike:

agree:

disagree:

don't get it:

---

think

- What is the core issue of the conflict in this story?
- Would you rather have Mary or Martha as an employee? Why?
- What are the advantages and disadvantages of being a "Mary"? Of being a "Martha"?

- In what ways does being a Mary come naturally to you? In what ways does being a Martha come naturally to you?

pray

read Your Personality and Your Work

From "You've Got Personality: Let It Guide You to the Right Business" by Pamela Rohland[2]

You may have a passion for entrepreneurship, but if you don't take your core personality traits into account, your new venture could be destined for failure.

"Your personality traits will help you select the best industry," says Marc Becker, a business psychologist in Anaheim Hills, California, "and that will help you weather adversity during the start-up process."

Here are common personality types and their best business bets.

Social Butterfly

Not content in an office in front of a computer or working solo from home, you'll be happiest out among clients and colleagues. You'd likely flourish in sales, teaching or consulting businesses that require interaction. Consider any business that involves networking, marketing and interacting.

- Party-energizing service (people who pose as party guests and mingle at social events, creating interesting conversation, getting people to dance and so on)
- Real estate sales
- Catering
- Management or executive recruiting
- Public relations or marketing
- Mobile DJ

Loner

Is working from the privacy of home your dream scenario? Then an e-business is your ideal option—and you don't need to be technologically sophisticated to get an online business going. But you need to be a good decision-maker, self-sufficient and able to play multiple roles.

- Web site selling gardening tools, baseball cards, cookies—choose your product
- Lifestyle Web site
- House- and plant-sitting

- Chauffeur service
- Web site design

Nurturer

You feel best when helping others. Many entrepreneurs who don't have strictly "nurturing" businesses are satisfied with nurturing and mentoring employees, but nurturers sometimes allow themselves to be taken advantage of, so balance the nurturing with toughness and authority.

- Massage therapist
- Senior care
- Restaurant selling comfort foods such as peanut butter and jelly sandwiches, meat loaf and mashed potatoes

Early Riser

Up before the sun? Being early is a trait most entrepreneurs would love to have. Consider a business that provides products or services to help those who get a later start.

- Breakfast restaurant or food cart offering customers eye-opening drinks and entrees
- Morning transportation service to make sure clients' children get to school or day care
- Newspaper abstracting service for companies (reading newspapers and writing brief summaries of the key articles to keep busy clients well informed of breaking events)
- Early pickup and delivery service
- Wake-up call service

Night Owl

Night owls do well in homebased businesses, independent consultant roles, and computer and Internet-related services allowing them to work when they're most productive: in the wee hours.

- Customer service center
- Security service
- After-hours dance club, book or video store, cybercafe, etc.
- Food-service business targeting late-shift manufacturing or service operations
- Secretarial or administrative support services

Worrier

Unpredictable income and uncertainties about the future will be stressful. Try making a gradual transition from full-time employment to entrepreneurship, and focus on low-risk ventures. Consider businesses that will lessen your own anxiety.

- Yoga school
- Manufacturer or marketer of stress-reduction products (aromatherapy, massage oils, worry beads, relaxation tapes)

Hyper-Energetic

You're best-suited to fast-paced, challenging and constantly changing activities. Businesses that require physical exertion and travel are also a good match for you. But stay away from solo work-at-home options.

- Child photographer
- Adventure-travel coordinator
- Personal trainer
- Telemarketer
- Firm that organizes and coaches pep rallies at large group events
- Training service

first thoughts

like:

dislike:

agree:

disagree:

don't get it:

think

- Make a list of the people in your discussion group and next to each name write the personality type that you think best describes that person. Share your thoughts about each other during your discussion time.
- How accurate are others' descriptions of you?
- Which personality type do you think best describes you? Which of the jobs listed in the article sound the most interesting to you? Which sound the least interesting? What is stopping you from learning more about the jobs you naturally like?
- Should your personality type be a factor in deciding the profession or career you will pursue? Why or why not?

pray

read Wholly Alive and Accepted

Romans 12:3-8

I'm speaking to you out of deep gratitude for all that God has given me, and especially as I have responsibilities in relation to you. Living then, as every one of you does, in pure grace, it's important that you not misinterpret yourselves as people who are bringing this goodness to God. No, God brings it all to you. The only accurate way to understand ourselves is by what God is and by what he does for us, not by what we are and what we do for him.

In this way we are like the various parts of a human body. Each part gets its meaning from the body as a whole, not the other way around. The body we're talking about is Christ's body of chosen people. Each of us finds our meaning and function as a part of his body. But as a chopped-off finger or cut-off toe we wouldn't amount to much, would we? So since we find ourselves fashioned into all these excellently formed and marvelously functioning parts in Christ's body, let's just go ahead and be what we were made to be, without enviously or pridefully comparing ourselves with each other, or trying to be something we aren't.

If you preach, just preach God's Message, nothing else; if you help, just help, don't take over; if you teach, stick to your teaching; if you give encouraging guidance, be careful that you don't get bossy; if you're put in charge, don't manipulate; if you're called to give aid to people in distress, keep your eyes open and be quick to respond; if you work with the disadvantaged, don't let yourself get irritated with them or depressed by them. Keep a smile on your face.

---

first thoughts

like:

dislike:

agree:

disagree:

don't get it:

---

think

- Why is it so hard to "go ahead and be what we were made to be"?
- In what ways are you tempted to cut off parts of your unique personality in order to fit in? In what ways are you tempted to cut off other people from being who they truly are?
- Do you have a tendency to underestimate or overestimate your self-worth?
- What steps can you take to see yourself as God sees you?

pray

read

From "Improve Your Employees' Job Satisfaction"[3]

The tough job market of the past two years has made life very difficult for those who are either unemployed or underemployed. And so you might think that your employees, because they have jobs, would be ecstatic. They aren't. While no doubt grateful for a paycheck, U.S. workers are actually less satisfied than they've been in many years.

A November 2003 survey by CareerBuilder, a leading job-search Web site, documents the extent of this dissatisfaction. The survey found that nearly one in four workers are now dissatisfied with their jobs, a 20 percent increase over 2001 levels, with some six out of ten workers planning to leave their current employer for other pursuits within the next two years. A similar survey by the Society for Human Resource Professionals revealed that more than eight out of ten workers intend to look for a new job when the economy heats up.

As an employer, you have good reason to be concerned about findings like these. A recent Ernst & Young survey calculated that the cost of replacing a high-level employee may be as much as 150 percent of that departing employee's salary. And matters could become worse very quickly. While the economy continues to rebound, existing workers will find job-hopping an increasingly viable option. And if predictions of widespread worker shortages by the latter half of the decade come true, these conditions will only be exacerbated.

How should you respond to this impending exodus of valuable workers? . . .

- **Provide workers with responsibility—and then let them use it.** Most surveys show that the greatest source of employee pride and satisfaction is the feeling of accomplishment that comes from having—and exercising—responsibility. Yet many business owners, consumed by fears of a shrinking bottom line, have turned micromanagement into an art form. Unfortunately, few things employers do cause more employee dissatisfaction. Here's the real bottom line: If you can't trust your employees to be able to think and act on their own, you probably shouldn't have hired them in the first place.

- **Show respect.** Frustrated by a faltering economy, diminishing markets and meddling investors, many business owners look close to home for someone to blame—all too often, that's their own employees. The result? A growing number of employees feel like they're being viewed as the enemy, not as loyal partners. It's little wonder so many workers seem ready to jump ship at the first sign of opportunity. On the other hand, companies that truly value their employees earn more than gratitude—they win enhanced dedication and productivity as well. So be sure to show your employees how much you respect and value them—tell them how much you appreciate them, throw them a pizza party, recognize an employee of the month, do anything you can to show them how much you care.

- **Recognize the whole person.** Employees are more than 9-to-5 robots who turn off at night and can't wait until the starting bell rings the next morning. All workers have lives, interests, and friends and family outside the office—and most are constantly struggling to balance increasingly hectic schedules. While companies can't sacrifice unduly to the whims of a single individual, making concessions where possible—allowing a long lunch break to attend a child's school event, for instance, or permitting a sales executive to fly out on Monday morning instead of Sunday night—can pay huge dividends in the long run.

- **Mark out a clear path to growth.** Some employees are content to remain where they are in an organization,

---

first thoughts

like:

dislike:

agree:

disagree:

don't get it:

but most want to grow in their careers over time. While annual performance reviews were originally designed to promote this goal, too often they have become empty, "Dilbertized" rituals, more embarrassing than ennobling. By contrast, business owners who wish to increase worker satisfaction tend to look past formalities and establish genuine growth paths for all their employees, not just their senior executives.

think

- Why do you think so many people are dissatisfied with their jobs? In which of your previous jobs have you been the most satisfied? The least satisfied? What made the difference?
- Which of the tactics listed in this article would have the biggest impact on improving your job satisfaction? Which would have the least impact?
- What motivates you to work? What motivates you to go above and beyond for an employer? How is this reflective of your personality?

pray

live   The Redefining

Take a few moments to skim through the notes you've made in these readings. What do they tell you about your personality? Based on what you've read and discussed, is there anything you want to change? Is there anything you need to accept?

What, if anything, is stopping you from making this change?

Are you allowing anyone or anything to define who you really are and what you really believe? If so, who or what is defining you? What are the results of that in your life? Do you need to make a change?

In what ways do you see your personality being molded by Christ in real time? In what areas of your life are you living as the world defines you?

Talk with a close friend about all of the above. Brainstorm together about what it might take to move toward God in this area of your life. Determine what this looks like in a practical sense and then list any measurable goals you want to shoot for here. Review these goals each week to see how you're doing.

realities
of the
workplace

I long to accomplish a great and noble task; but
it is my chief duty to accomplish small tasks as
if they were great and noble.

Helen Keller

a reminder

*Before you dive into this study, spend a little time reviewing what
you wrote in the previous lessons' Live sections. How are you doing?
Check with your small-group members and review your progress
toward the specified goals. If necessary, adjust your goals and plans
and then recommit to them.*

the defining line

Adjusting to the working world can be a little rough. The working world is
filled with a long list of challenges, from office politics and poor management to conflict between personnel, all of which can be tough waters to
navigate.

What has surprised you most about the working world? How have
you responded to these surprises? In what ways are you still dealing with
them?

What are some of the biggest challenges you have faced in your current and previous jobs? Now dig a little deeper. What have you discovered about yourself through those challenges? Are there any lessons you're still in the process of learning?

Consider sharing your responses with your group when you meet.

read Life in a Cube

From *How to Be a Grown-Up: 247 Lab-Tested Strategies for Conquering the World* by Margaret Feinberg and Leif Oines[1]

After being in school, having an entire cubicle as "yours" is quite a step up. At least it may seem like that for the first couple of weeks . . .

Of course, while you are still going through orientation and OJT (on-the-job training), you will have plenty of time to decorate with an eye toward sensibility, an expression of your personality, and comfort. So during your first week of work, you raid your photo albums and make frequent visits to business supply stores and the mall to pick up the following:

- Photos of graduation—*reminders that you really do belong here in the real world*
- Snapshots of friends and family—*these are the important people in your life*
- A bowl of potpourri—*the air seems a little stale*
- Fun little conversation starters—*these are cool little trolls with big hair, don't you think?*
- Special folders of different types of paper products—*you'll probably need a bunch of different paper for difficult projects*
- The coolest pens you can afford in every color made—*rubberized grip, gel rollerballs that write upside down in space*
- Post-it notes in every color and shape—*this way you can keep track of everything*
- A brand-new Rolodex—*for all the new people you'll be meeting*
- A great calendar with M. C. Escher prints—*pretty amazing how those steps keep going up!*

After decorating your new workspace, then you can finally get down to changing the world with an out-of-date computer and rotary dial telephone.

And the weeks go by . . .

After ten weeks of work, you look around and realize that your cubicle seems to have shrunk. Ten weeks ago you remember measuring it for a rug that you never purchased and found that it was a very open and spacious eight feet by eight feet. Figuring that one of your coworkers is messing with you, you measure it again and it actually is the same eight by eight square. But something is different . . .

- You look around and recognize things are definitely different from when you started work.
- The photos of graduation have disappeared since you realized the folks around you aren't impressed by your *I've-never-heard-of-that-school-before* diploma.
- Snapshots of friends and family have been removed because there are some real weirdos in your office and you don't want to give them clues about where you live or those you love.
- The bowl of potpourri has been exchanged for numerous tree-shaped air fresheners since you can hang them around your neck, which helps you deal with the smelly guy in the next cubicle over who doesn't shower regularly.
- Those fun little conversation starters are in a desk drawer because you don't really want to talk to your coworkers unless you have to.
- All the special folders of different types of paper products have been given to scrap-booking because you haven't had a different project since you began working at the company months ago.
- The coolest pens you could afford have disappeared. They were on your desk when you left work Friday and were gone when you returned to the office Monday morning.
- The Post-it notes in every shape and color became an anniversary gift for your girlfriend since the only thing you need to remember for work is basic data entry.
- The Rolodex was helpful, at least for the box it came in. Putting your data entry spreadsheets on top of it has made your desk seem bigger.
- The great calendar with M. C. Escher prints has been replaced with a basic office calendar since your boss said that trying to figure out how the steps kept going up made him dizzy and you needed to take it home.

Oh well, you think. *That's my life in a cube.*

first thoughts

like:

dislike:

agree:

disagree:

don't get it:

think

- This article highlights some of the struggles of adjusting to the nine-to-five. Describe any parts of your job that make you feel like you're living in a cube. In what ways do you think your job helps you grow as a person? In what ways do you think it limits your personal growth?
- What advice would you give to someone who is transitioning from full-time student to full-time employee?
- What is the most challenging part of your job? What are you doing to step up to the challenge?

pray

read A Difficult Boss

Daniel 1

It was the third year of King Jehoiakim's reign in Judah when King Nebuchadnezzar of Babylon declared war on Jerusalem and besieged the city. The Master handed King Jehoiakim of Judah over to him, along with some of the furnishings from the Temple of God. Nebuchadnezzar took king and furnishings to the country of Babylon, the ancient Shinar. He put the furnishings in the sacred treasury.

The king told Ashpenaz, head of the palace staff, to get some Israelites from the royal family and nobility—young men who were healthy and handsome, intelligent and well-educated, good prospects for leadership positions in the government, perfect specimens!—and indoctrinate them in the Babylonian language and the lore of magic and fortunetelling. The king then ordered that they be served from the same menu as the royal table—the best food, the finest wine. After three years of training they would be given positions in the king's court.

Four young men from Judah—Daniel, Hananiah, Mishael, and Azariah—were among those selected. The head of the palace staff gave them Babylonian names: Daniel was named Belteshazzar, Hananiah was named Shadrach, Mishael was named Meshach, Azariah was named Abednego.

But Daniel determined that he would not defile himself by eating the king's food or drinking his wine, so he asked the head of the palace staff to exempt him from the royal diet. The head of the palace staff, by God's grace, liked Daniel, but he warned him, "I'm afraid of what my master the king will do. He is the one who assigned this diet and if he sees that you are not as healthy as the rest, he'll have my head!"

But Daniel appealed to a steward who had been assigned by the head of the palace staff to be in charge of Daniel, Hananiah, Mishael, and Azariah: "Try us out for ten days on a simple diet of vegetables and water. Then compare us with the young men who eat from the royal menu. Make your decision on the basis of what you see."

The steward agreed to do it and fed them vegetables and water for ten days. At the end of the ten days they looked better and more robust than all the others who had been eating from the royal menu. So the steward continued to exempt them from the royal menu of food and drink and served them only vegetables.

God gave these four young men knowledge and skill in both books and life. In addition, Daniel was gifted in understanding all sorts of visions and dreams. At the end of the time set by the king for their training, the head of the royal staff brought them in to Nebuchadnezzar. When the king interviewed them, he found them far superior to all the other young men. None were a match for Daniel, Hananiah, Mishael, and Azariah.

And so they took their place in the king's service. Whenever the king consulted them on anything, on books or on life, he found them ten times better than all the magicians and enchanters in his kingdom put together.

Daniel continued in the king's service until the first year in the reign of King Cyrus.

---

first thoughts

like:

dislike:

agree:

disagree:

don't get it:

---

think

- Do you think King Nebuchadnezzar could be classified as a tough boss? Why or why not? What made him so difficult?
- What lessons can be learned from this passage about how to handle a difficult boss?
- Do you think Daniel, Hananiah, Mishael, or Azariah would have been able to handle the situation as well if they had been on their own instead of united? Why or why not?
- Why is the fellowship of like-minded believers so important, even in a work environment?
- Describe your most difficult boss. What made working for this person so difficult? What did you do to try to resolve the situation?

pray

read Plagued by Self-Doubt

Exodus 4:1-18

Moses objected, "They won't trust me. They won't listen to a word I say. They're going to say, 'GOD? Appear to him? Hardly!'"

So GOD said, "What's that in your hand?"

"A staff."

"Throw it on the ground." He threw it. It became a snake; Moses jumped back—fast!

GOD said to Moses, "Reach out and grab it by the tail." He reached out and grabbed it—and he was holding his staff again. "That's so they will trust that GOD appeared to you, the God of their fathers, the God of Abraham, the God of Isaac, and the God of Jacob."

GOD then said, "Put your hand inside your shirt." He slipped his hand under his shirt, then took it out. His hand had turned leprous, like snow.

He said, "Put your hand back under your shirt." He did it, then took it back out—as healthy as before.

"So if they don't trust you and aren't convinced by the first sign, the second sign should do it. But if it doesn't, if even after these two signs they don't trust you and listen to your message, take some water out of the Nile and pour it out on the dry land; the Nile water that you pour out will turn to blood when it hits the ground."

Moses raised another objection to GOD: "Master, please, I don't talk well. I've never been good with words, neither before nor after you spoke to me. I stutter and stammer."

GOD said, "And who do you think made the human mouth? And who makes some mute, some deaf, some sighted, some blind? Isn't it I, GOD? So, get going. I'll be right there with you—with your mouth! I'll be right there to teach you what to say."

He said, "Oh, Master, please! Send somebody else!"

GOD got angry with Moses: "Don't you have a brother, Aaron the Levite? He's good with words, I know he is. He speaks very well. In fact, at this very moment he's on his way to meet you. When he sees you he's going to be glad. You'll speak to him and tell him what to say. I'll be right there with you as you speak and with him as he speaks, teaching you step by step. He will speak to the people for you. He'll act as your mouth, but you'll decide what comes out of it. Now take this staff in your hand; you'll use it to do the signs."

Moses went back to Jethro his father-in-law and said, "I need to return to my relatives who are in Egypt. I want to see if they're still alive."

Jethro said, "Go. And peace be with you."

---

first thoughts

like:

dislike:

agree:

disagree:

don't get it:

---

think

- Do you doubt yourself at work? How does your doubt undermine your performance?
- In what ways do you feel called to your current job? In what ways do you feel called to another job? What are you doing to fulfill the calling on your life?
- Have you, like Moses, been arguing with God about the calling on your life? Explain.
- Is there anyone at work who could become a mentor to help you grow professionally? Is there anyone you could mentor? What is stopping you from developing these relationships?

pray

read Seeing Through the Glass Ceiling

From "Identify Your Glass Ceiling and Attain True Workplace Diversity"[2]

What is the Glass Ceiling?

The term "glass ceiling" first entered America's public lexicon in 1986 when *The Wall Street Journal*'s "Corporate Woman" column identified a puzzling new phenomenon. There seemed to be an invisible—but impenetrable—barrier between women and the executive suite, preventing them from reaching the highest levels of the business world regardless of their accomplishments and merits. The phrase immediately captured the attention of the public as well as business leaders, journalists, and policy makers. The metaphor was quickly extended to refer to obstacles hindering the advancement of minorities as well as women.

The glass ceiling is defined by the Department of Labor as those artificial barriers based on attitudinal or organizational bias that prevent qualified individuals from advancing in their organization into upper management positions. These artificial barriers may exist in seemingly neutral hiring criteria, or in the selection criteria used for advancement and professional development opportunities. These same barriers may also prevent minority men and women of all races from being given assignments that can lead to the development of expertise and credibility. The existence of the glass ceiling ultimately results in reduced participation by minority men and women of all races in executive management positions in corporations. Where the glass ceiling exists, white women—and minority men and women in greater numbers— are relegated to lower paying

first thoughts

like:

dislike:

agree:

disagree:

don't get it:

positions. This is costly to corporations both economically and in terms of damaging morale. It can lead to an inability to recruit talented professionals, increased turnover and the loss of highly skilled talent in which many corporations have made major investments. The increasingly "non-traditional" look of the current workforce requires that corporations value minority men and women of all races and provide them with developmental opportunities. The Department of Labor's Glass Ceiling Initiative is an effort to identify and help remedy this problem facing America's workforce.

think

- Have you ever encountered a glass ceiling? If so, describe the situation. How did you respond? How should Christians respond to glass ceilings?
- How can a glass ceiling undermine an employee's performance and contribution to a company?
- What can employees do to help employers recognize and remove glass ceilings?

pray

read Sources of Conflict

Luke 9:46-48

They started arguing over which of them would be most famous. When Jesus realized how much this mattered to them, he brought a child to his side. "Whoever accepts this child as if the child were me, accepts me," he said. "And whoever accepts me, accepts the One who sent me. You become great by accepting, not asserting. Your spirit, not your size, makes the difference."

---

first thoughts

like:

dislike:

agree:

disagree:

don't get it:

---

think

- What are some sources of conflict in a workplace? What can you do to minimize the amount of conflict where you work?
- How do you know when it's appropriate to stand up for an issue at work and when it's better to let it go?
- Is there a point when it's right to speak up and potentially create conflict at work? If so, explain.

- Respond to this statement: "You become great by accepting, not asserting." In what ways is this true in a work environment? In what ways does it not apply?

pray

live   The Redefining

Take a few moments to skim through the notes you've made in these readings. What do they reveal about your attitudes toward work? What do they reveal about your attitudes toward your coworkers and boss? Based on what you've read and discussed, is there anything you want to change?

What, if anything, is stopping you from making this change?

In what ways could you be a better worker? In what ways could you be a better reflection of Christ in your workplace?

Are there any areas of your job that you've neglected to pray about? If so, write out a prayer below.

Talk with a close friend about all of the above. Brainstorm together about what it might take to move toward God in this area of your life. Determine what this looks like in a practical sense and then list any measurable goals you want to shoot for here. Review these goals each week to see how you're doing.

interpersonal
challenges

Real wisdom, God's wisdom, begins with a holy life
and is characterized by getting along with others. It is gentle and reasonable, overflowing with
mercy and blessings, not hot one day and cold the
next, not two-faced. You can develop a healthy,
robust community that lives right with God and
enjoy its results *only* if you do the hard work of
getting along with each other, treating each other
with dignity and honor.

James 3:17-18

a reminder

*Before you dive into this study, spend a little time reviewing what
you wrote in the previous lessons' Live sections. How are you doing?
Check with your small-group members and review your progress
toward the specified goals. If necessary, adjust your goals and plans
and then recommit to them.*

the defining line

You may get to pick your friends, but you don't always have that luxury when
it comes to your fellow employees. You may have hundreds or thousands of
coworkers at your job, or you may just have a handful. Either way, there are
bound to be interpersonal issues that arise from working together.

It's easy to point out the faults and shortcomings of fellow employees,
but have you ever taken time to reflect on yourself as an employee? What

are you like to work with? On a scale of one to ten, how agreeable (one) or disagreeable (ten) are you when it comes to working together on projects with others? Record and explain your response below.

In what areas of your work are you tempted to be a know-it-all? Are there any areas in which you're difficult to work with? What steps do you need to take to maintain a more humble attitude?

In what areas of your job is it easier to keep a humble attitude?

Develop a short game plan for becoming a better employee. Consider sharing your plan, along with your other responses, with your group when you meet.

read Ending the War

From "Working Wounded: Conflict Resolution: Handling Conflicts with Co-Workers" by Bob Rosner[1]

QUESTION: I've been battling with a co-worker for a long time. I'd like to end the conflict once and for all. Can you tell me how?

ANSWER: Your e-mail reminded me of a conflict of biblical proportions that I recently heard about. At the New Salem Missionary Baptist Church the parishioners voted 67-10 to fire their pastor Stanley Hall. His crime? He refused to reschedule a consecration service that conflicted with the Super Bowl.

Pastor Hall learned the hard way that a little bit of flexibility goes a long way toward keeping people happy. It's no different when dealing with conflict at work. I've listed strategies below to help you take your conflict with your co-worker to a better place.

Tips for improving relations

Do you try to see the world through their eyes? As my mom was fond of saying, it takes two to tango. So take a moment to explore how you contribute to the problem with your co-worker. Then try to see the world through the eyes of the other person. What pressures, history and politics are influencing their actions/behaviors?

Ask, "Can we sit down and work this out?" Conflict's great enabler is the 10-foot pole. You've got to get up close and personal with the person you're having problems with to see if it's possible to hash out your issues. There is, perhaps unfortunately, no such thing as "long distance" conflict resolution.

Do you thank the other person for agreeing to meet? Don't ever take for granted that they agreed to talk with you. Let them know that you appreciate it.

Do you use "I" statements? It's common when you are angry with someone to use a lot of "you" statements, like "you left early while the rest of us worked late." This tends to make the other person defensive and tends to block your ability to work together toward a solution. That's why it's important to use "I" statements like "I feel frustrated with how late Jim

is having to work" to let them know what you're feeling without needlessly
raising their hackles.

---

first thoughts

like:

dislike:

agree:

disagree:

don't get it:

---

think

- Are there any coworkers you've had an ongoing struggle with?
  What is the core issue of the struggle for you personally? What
  prevents you from letting it go and moving on?
- Are there certain situations that create unavoidable conflict in
  your job? How do you respond?
- How should a Christian respond to conflict?
- Which of the tips described in this article have you tried? Which
  worked? Which didn't?

pray

read Separate Ways

cts 15:36-41

After a few days of this, Paul said to Barnabas, "Let's go back and visit all our friends in each of the towns where we preached the Word of God. Let's see how they're doing."

Barnabas wanted to take John along, the John nicknamed Mark. But Paul wouldn't have him; he wasn't about to take along a quitter who, as soon as the going got tough, had jumped ship on them in Pamphylia. Tempers flared, and they ended up going their separate ways: Barnabas took Mark and sailed for Cyprus; Paul chose Silas and, offered up by their friends to the grace of the Master, went to Syria and Cilicia to build up muscle and sinew in those congregations.

---

first thoughts

like:

dislike:

agree:

disagree:

don't get it:

---

think

- What, if anything, about this passage surprises you?
- Do you think conflict, even among Christians, is unavoidable? Why or why not?

- In what ways do you think Paul and Barnabas responded to each other in a Christlike manner? Do you think their response to each other could have been better? If so, how?
- How would you have responded if you were Paul or Barnabas?

pray

LESSON 4: INTERPERSONAL CHALLENGES   65

read "Blessed" from 9 to 5?

Matthew 5:1-9

When Jesus saw his ministry drawing huge crowds, he climbed a hillside. Those who were apprenticed to him, the committed, climbed with him. Arriving at a quiet place, he sat down and taught his climbing companions. This is what he said:

"You're blessed when you're at the end of your rope. With less of you there is more of God and his rule.

"You're blessed when you feel you've lost what is most dear to you. Only then can you be embraced by the One most dear to you.

"You're blessed when you're content with just who you are—no more, no less. That's the moment you find yourselves proud owners of everything that can't be bought.

"You're blessed when you've worked up a good appetite for God. He's food and drink in the best meal you'll ever eat.

"You're blessed when you care. At the moment of being 'care-full,' you find yourselves cared for.

"You're blessed when you get your inside world—your mind and heart—put right. Then you can see God in the outside world.

---

first thoughts

like:

dislike:

agree:

disagree:

don't get it:

---

redefininglife

"You're blessed when you can show people how to cooperate instead of compete or fight. That's when you discover who you really are, and your place in God's family."

think

- What does this passage reveal about how you should respond to others at work? Which of the statements is the easiest to follow? Which is the most difficult?
- Do you feel like you "can show people how to cooperate instead of compete or fight" at work? Why or why not? What keeps you from doing this more often?
- What prevents you from being more "blessed" in your workplace? In your relationships outside of work?

pray

read The Guide to Office Politics

From "The Good Guy's (and Gal's) Guide to Office Politics" by Michael Warshaw[2]

When Cindy Casselman took a communications job at Xerox headquarters in Stamford, Connecticut, the company's communications weren't so good. If Xerox made a big acquisition or had a disappointing quarter, many of its 85,000 people read the news in the papers before they got the scoop from the company. Casselman was determined to change things. "I was manager of employee communications," she says. "I took my job seriously."

But Casselman, now 50, didn't have much formal authority. She was, to use an out-of-favor phrase, a middle manager: someone whose boss had a boss who had a boss. So she assembled a makeshift budget and mustered a volunteer team that she called the Sanctioned Covert Operation (SCO)—"sanctioned," because her direct boss tolerated what looked like a modest project; "covert," because her actual goals were more ambitious than she let on.

Today, thanks to the SCO, any Xerox employee can visit the WebBoard, the company's spirited intranet site, and talk to other employees, read up-to-the-minute news about internal developments—and in general get more connected to what's happening inside this vast enterprise. How did Casselman have such a big impact with so few resources? She had a knack for playing politics.

Chris Newell, 47, is founder and executive director of Lotus Institute, a 20-member unit of Lotus Development Corp. (based in Cambridge, Massachusetts) that develops solutions using Lotus Notes software. It's a fun and interesting job—but hardly a position of power. "We generate new ideas about how software interacts with culture," he says. "We're the shrinks of shrinkwrap."

Last year, Newell became convinced that the emerging field of "knowledge management" represented a big market opportunity for Lotus and its parent company, IBM. So he became a major catalyst behind a series of knowledge-management products that Lotus and IBM began to roll out by the end of the year. Newell didn't have the authority to order such initiatives. But he did know how to play politics.

About three and a half years ago, when the *Discovery Channel* wanted to extend its high-profile brand beyond cable TV, CEO John Hendricks assembled a committee to explore interactive television. Tom Hicks, now 44, thought the company should focus on the Internet. But this was 1994, when pundits were heralding interactive TV and the Net was still an unproven medium. Worse, Hicks ran the division that produced *Discovery*'s magazines. Today the *Discovery Channel Online* is a much-celebrated presence on the Web. And when was the last time you watched interactive TV? Pushing for this mid-course correction wasn't easy. It meant playing politics.

Office politics. Just say the words, and you sense the disdain. Isn't "playing politics" a tool for people who can't get ahead on merit—who pursue their own agenda regardless of what's good for their colleagues or the company? That's the downside of office politics. But what about the upside? Office politics is a lot like "real" politics. Plenty of politicians launch campaigns simply because they relish the privileges of power. But at least some politicians campaign for things that matter to people other than themselves. Dismissing all political campaigns as cynical and self-aggrandizing becomes a self-fulfilling prophecy. The same goes for office politics.

"When people talk about office politics, they usually mean something dirty or underhanded," says management professor Allan Cohen, dean of faculty at Babson College and coauthor of *Influence Without Authority* (John Wiley & Sons, 1991). "But nobody exists in an atmosphere where everybody agrees. Politics is the art of trying to accomplish things within organizations."

Marilyn Moats Kennedy, a career coach based in Wilmette, Illinois, claims that the underlying logic of office politics is changing—and opening the door to campaigners who want to get things done rather than do other people in. "Workers today," she says, "compete for schedules and projects, for money and training. But they

first thoughts

like:

dislike:

agree:

disagree:

don't get it:

rarely compete for power—especially when that means power over others. Instead of power, people want assignments that build skills valued by the market. Learning experiences are what's really important."

Herminia Ibarra, an associate professor at the Harvard Business School who teaches a popular course called "Power and Influence," offers yet another perspective on office politics: You don't have to be a jerk to make things happen. "Integrity," she says, "can be a source of power."

think

- Do you think office politics are unavoidable? Why or why not?
- Try to think of three situations in which you played office politics in your current or previous jobs. What was the result?
- Do you think there's an upside to office politics? Explain. Do you think it's possible to avoid the downside of office politics? Explain.
- Respond to this statement: "Integrity . . . can be a source of power." In what ways do you think that's true?

pray

read Being Happy for Others

From "Wishing Well" by Sharon Salzberg[3]

I recently visited a friend in Malibu, a spectacularly beautiful beach town north of Los Angeles. As I walked along the sand, I was captivated by the warm breeze, the sound of the ocean, and the light glinting off the water. Glancing at the luxurious houses lining the shore, I imagined that this was as good as it gets.

Then the rains came. Hour after hour, day after day, rain pounded down. My friend's garage roof leaked. The stuff she was storing there all had to be moved. When the storm was over, battalions of ants marched through her kitchen. In the midst of the chaos, a national news correspondent called and asked if she could come out with a television crew to film the scene. Puzzled, my friend asked, "Why?" The woman replied, "Well, all around the country people get excited if they hear that something's gone wrong in Malibu."

We relish others' misfortunes when we begrudge them their apparent happiness. Hearing about another person's success, we might think, "Oooh. I would be happier if you had just a little bit less going for you right now. You don't have to lose everything, of course; just a slight tarnishing of that glow would be nice." We react as though good fortune were a limited commodity, so the more someone else has, the less there will be for us. As we watch someone else partake of the stockpile of joy, our hearts may

---

first thoughts

like:

dislike:

agree:

disagree:

don't get it:

---

sink—we're not going to get our share. But someone else's pleasure doesn't cause our unhappiness—we make ourselves unhappy because our negativity isolates us.

think

- Under what circumstances do you struggle to celebrate the good fortune of others?
- What does Jesus say about celebrating the good fortune of others? Why is it important? What happens when you celebrate with someone else?
- Is jealousy ever an issue for you at work? If so, describe how.
- What can you do to build healthier, more Christlike relationships with your coworkers? What is stopping you from building those relationships?

pray

live   The Redefining

Take a few moments to skim through the notes you've made in these readings. What do they tell you about how you're responding to the challenges you face at work? Based on what you've read and discussed, is there anything you want to change?

What, if anything, is stopping you from making this change?

Make a list of the three biggest personnel struggles you've experienced at work. One by one, talk through each of them with God. Share at least one with the members of your group.

In what ways are you responding with Christlikeness to your challenges at work? How are you responding in ways that do not reflect Christ? What do you need to change?

Talk with a close friend about all of the above. Brainstorm together about what it might take to move toward God in this area of your life. Determine what this looks like in a practical sense and then list any measurable goals you want to shoot for here. Review these goals each week to see how you're doing.

identity
and the
workplace

You know me inside and out, you know every bone in my
body; You know exactly how I was made, bit by bit,
how I was sculpted from nothing into something.

Psalm 139:15

a reminder

*Before you dive into this study, spend a little time reviewing what
you wrote in the previous lessons' Live sections. How are you doing?
Check with your small-group members and review your progress
toward the specified goals. If necessary, adjust your goals and plans
and then recommit to them.*

the defining line

How do you discover who you really are? Ask the One who made you. God
knows you better than you know yourself. In Him you are given your true
identity as a child of God. Unfortunately, it's far too easy to seek out our
identity and try to find context for our existence in the temporal things of this
world. It's easy to let our family, our friends, and even our jobs define us.

In the space below, write a short paragraph describing yourself. Pretend
your name is a word in the dictionary. What would the definition be?

Share this definition with the members of your group and ask them to add to the definition what they know about you. Write their additions in the space below.

Now, reflecting on the completed definition, how much does your work or what you want to do with your life define who you are?

Consider sharing your answer with your group when you meet.

read The Changing Nature of a Job

From *What the Heck Am I Going to Do with My Life? Pursue Your Passion, Find the Answer* by Margaret Feinberg[1]

Whether you realize it or not, a dramatic change has taken place in the workplace over the last twenty to thirty years. For previous generations, a job was just that—a job. You put in your hours and earned your pay. A good job was a good *paying* job. But as the pace of life and length of the workweek has continued to increase, more and more people are looking to their workplace to provide more than just a paycheck. Today's dream job provides meaning, purpose, and authentic community. It fosters personal growth, develops individual talents and allows you to make our planet a little better at the end of the day. And, oh yeah, it allows you to pay back all those student loans (ahead of schedule) and afford a little bling-bling or at least a really nice vacation with friends on a tropical beach. In other words, a job title twenty years ago was a reflection of what you did. A job title today is now a reflection of who you are.

---

first thoughts

like:

dislike:

agree:

disagree:

don't get it:

---

think

- Besides a paycheck, what does your work mean to you? What unspoken expectations do you place on your job?
- Underline all the things listed in this passage that a job can provide. Which of these things is your current job providing? Which do you wish your current job provided?
- Respond to this statement: "A job title twenty years ago was a reflection of what you did. A job title today is now a reflection of who you are." In what ways do you identify with the statement? In what ways do you think it's false?
- In what ways do you find your identity in your job? Do you think you have a healthy perspective on this? Why or why not?

pray

read Your Job and You

From "Are You Your Job?" by Peter Doskoch[2]

When you mess up at work, are you inspired to re-group, or do your spirits and performance plummet? If your job is important to your identity, your answer will depend on whether you're given the chance to redeem yourself.

German researchers Joachim Brunstein, Ph.D., and Peter Gollwitzer, Ph.D., asked 96 medical students, all highly committed to their careers, to complete a quiz that supposedly measured social skills. Then the future doctors were asked to tackle a test that required quickly scanning a text for apostrophes.

Some of the students were led to believe that both tests assessed abilities vital to medical success, and that they had done poorly on the first one. Because this bad news threatened their identities as budding doctors, they attacked the second exam with more gusto—and scored higher than any group in the study.

But another set of students, told that they'd botched the first test but that the second one did not reflect their career prospects, did far worse on the follow-up. The reason? While taking the second quiz, they were mulling over their initial failure rather than concentrating on the apostrophes, Brunstein and Gollwitzer report in the *Journal of Personality and Social Psychology.* So bosses seeking to inspire a staff to improve after setbacks will have more success if they give employees a chance to restore their damaged sense of self, rather than reassigning them to menial tasks.

first thoughts

like:

dislike:

agree:

disagree:

don't get it:

think

- In what ways does your perception of how well you're doing at work affect your work performance?
- How much positive feedback do you need at work? How much positive feedback do you offer to others on a regular basis?
- What can you do to give more encouragement and affirmation to fellow workers?
- Are you ever tempted to "beat yourself up" when you make a mistake at work? What effect does this have on your work?
- How can you break the cycle of being so hard on yourself?

pray

read   When What You Do Becomes Who You Are

From "Good Pastor, Lousy Leader: How I Came to Terms with My Role in the Church" by Matthew Woodley[3]

Five solemn-faced people assembled on the other side of the conference table, eyes averted. It was time for my performance review. Nobody seemed particularly festive.

For several months there had been rumblings about my pastoral "performance." Nobody doubted my gifts as a preacher or questioned my commitment to Christ. But everyone at the table that day knew there was a growing discontent with my skills as an administrator and leader. Still, I remained confident, ready to admit my faults and defend my record as their pastor.

A month earlier these members of our staff-parish relations committee had filled out an evaluation form, rating me on a scale from 1 ("needs a great deal of improvement") to 5 ("superior, excellent"). Now, everyone sat stiffly in their chairs, fidgeting with their completed evaluation forms.

Finally, to break the awkward silence, I volunteered to evaluate myself.

I gave myself 3's and 4's on most areas but rated myself a mere 2 ("needs some improvement") in leadership and administration.

"I confess that this area is not my strength," I said. "It's been a tough transition coming from a small church, but I'm willing to grow as your leader." How much more transparent and vulnerable can a pastor get? I thought to myself. Surely they'll have compassion, or at least pity, on me. They'll probably even insist that I be bumped up to a 3 ("fully satisfactory").

Billy, the senior member of the committee, tapped his pen and stared at his evaluation form. "Well, Pastor," he drawled, "actually I was thinking that a 2 was pretty high. As a leader and administrator, I gave you a 1."

I glanced at the full page of notes Billy had written in the comments section. "Poor communication . . . poor administration . . . confused leadership" were just some of the phrases that caught my eye.

"Billy, I don't think Pastor Matt is that bad as a leader," said a young woman named Janet. "I mean, if he was really that bad, the church would be falling apart."

Billy glared as if to say, "My point exactly."

After a half-hour of discussion, the committee agreed I wasn't quite bad enough to merit a 1. I squeaked by with a 2. . . .

Bad leader, bad person

The "good pastor, lousy leader" dilemma strikes at the root of my identity. It hooks my sense of shame. For me, it's a short slide from "I'm a poor leader" to "I'm an inadequate person" to "I'm a failure in my calling and therefore as a Christian."

My friend George pastors a booming church in the southeast. Mentored by some of the finest leaders in our denomination, George is a gifted leader and visionary. Church leadership issues are his passion. He devours books by Bill Hybels, John Maxwell, George Barna, and Rick Warren. George exudes confidence as a leader.

Whenever George shares about his church's growth, I don't feel angry; I just feel leadership-deficient. Why can't I lead a church like George? I say to myself. I devour books by C. S. Lewis, Feodor Dostoevsky, Richard Foster, and St. John of the Cross. Did I miss the leadership boat? Am I an incompetent pastor?

Amid this swirling sense of inadequacy, I phoned my pastoral mentor, 79-year-old C. Philip Hinerman, or as all his protégés call him, "Doc." For 37 years, Doc pastored Park Avenue United Methodist Church in the heart of Minneapolis. Today "Park" has a vibrant witness in the community, preaching the gospel and modeling Christ-centered racial reconciliation. But for nearly the first half of Doc's ministry, the church consistently lost members, dwindling from 1,400 in 1952 to 700 members in 1974.

I thought Doc would identify with my feelings of inadequacy, so I candidly asked him, "During those declining years at Park Avenue, did you ever feel like a failure as a leader?"

"Absolutely not," he said without hesitating. "My church situation, my 'success' as a leader, was never a spiritual issue. It really had nothing to do with my value as a minister or my walk with Christ. I was surrendered to Christ when I started my ministry, and I was just as surrendered to Christ when we lost a hundred members a year."

Doc's perspective helped me separate my leadership struggles from my identity in Christ. I had made it into a spiritual issue: I'm struggling as a leader; therefore I'm a spiritual failure. After my conversation with Doc, the suffocating feeling of inadequacy began to lift.

first thoughts

like:

dislike:

agree:

disagree:

don't get it:

think

- The author says, "For me, it's a short slide from 'I'm a poor leader' to 'I'm an inadequate person' to 'I'm a failure in my calling and therefore as a Christian.'" In what ways do you feel inadequate at work? In what ways do you feel inadequate in your spiritual life? Do you think there's a connection? Why or why not?
- Why do you think it's so easy to internalize the affirmation (or lack of affirmation) you receive through your work? What can you do to separate your identity from your work?
- What does success mean to you? Write a definition of success that is personal and specific for your life right now. In what ways are you living a successful life? What role does personal growth, including hard times, play in your definition of success?

pray

read Your Value and Identity

Philippians 3:2-16

Steer clear of the barking dogs, those religious busybodies, all bark and no bite. All they're interested in is appearances—knife-happy circumcisers, I call them. The *real* believers are the ones the Spirit of God leads to work away at this ministry, filling the air with Christ's praise as we do it. We couldn't carry this off by our own efforts, and we know it—even though we can list what many might think are impressive credentials. You know my pedigree: a legitimate birth, circumcised on the eighth day; an Israelite from the elite tribe of Benjamin; a strict and devout adherent to God's law; a fiery defender of the purity of my religion, even to the point of persecuting Christians; a meticulous observer of everything set down in God's law Book.

The very credentials these people are waving around as something special, I'm tearing up and throwing out with the trash—along with everything else I used to take credit for. And why? Because of Christ. Yes, all the things I once thought were so important are gone from my life. Compared to the high privilege of knowing Christ Jesus as my Master, firsthand, everything I once thought I had going for me is insignificant—dog dung. I've dumped it all in the trash so that I could embrace Christ and be embraced by him. I didn't want some petty, inferior brand of righteousness that comes from keeping a list of rules when I could get the robust kind that comes from trusting Christ—*God's* righteousness.

I gave up all that inferior stuff so I could know Christ personally, experience his resurrection power, be a partner in his suffering, and go all the way with him to death itself. If there was any way to get in on the resurrection from the dead, I wanted to do it.

I'm not saying that I have this all together, that I have it made. But I am well on my way, reaching out for Christ, who has so wondrously reached out for me. Friends, don't get me wrong: By no means do I count myself an expert in all of this, but I've got my eye on the goal, where God is beckoning us onward—to Jesus. I'm off and running, and I'm not turning back.

So let's keep focused on that goal, those of us who want everything God has for us. If any of you have something else in mind, something less than total commitment, God will clear your blurred vision—you'll see it yet! Now that we're on the right track, let's stay on it.

---

first thoughts

like:

dislike:

agree:

disagree:

don't get it:

---

think

- Why do you think so many people find their identity in their accomplishments and achievements? In what ways are you tempted to do this?
- How important are credentials to you in your estimation of other people? In your estimation of yourself? How much do you allow credentials to define other people? To define yourself?
- According to this passage, what is more important than credentials? What truly gives you value? Where should your identity come from?

pray

read Strong in Who You Are

From "Radio Host Prefers Class over Crass" by Skip Bayless[4]

Mark Cuban, owner of the NBA's Dallas Mavericks, recently offered WGN Chicago Radio sports-talk host David Kaplan $50,000 to change his name legally to "Dallas Maverick."

When Kaplan politely declined, Cuban sweetened the offer. Cuban would pay Kaplan $100,000 and donate $100,000 to Kaplan's favorite charity if he took the name for one year.

After some soul searching, and being bombarded by e-mails from listeners who said he was crazy to turn down the money, Kaplan held firm and told Cuban no. Kaplan explained: "I'd be saying I'd do anything for money and that bothers me. My name is my birthright. I'd like to preserve my integrity and credibility."

---

first thoughts

like:

dislike:

agree:

disagree:

don't get it:

---

think

- Would you change your name for $100,000? At what price would you change your name?

- Have you ever been placed in a situation in which your job has asked you to be who you're not? How did you handle the situation? How did others respond to the way you handled it?
- Have you ever been asked to compromise your integrity or values at your workplace? How did you respond?
- How can you maintain your identity in your job but still fulfill your responsibilities and requirements?

pray

live   The Redefining

Take a few moments to skim through the notes you've made in these readings. What do they reveal to you about where you find your identity? Do you think you have a healthy or unhealthy relationship with your job? Based on what you've read and discussed, is there anything you want to change?

What, if anything, is stopping you from making this change?

Are there any ways in which your job defines who you are? What steps can you take to have a more balanced life?

Talk with a close friend about all of the above. Brainstorm together about what it might take to move toward God in this area of your life. Determine what this looks like in a practical sense and then list any measurable goals you want to shoot for here. Review these goals each week to see how you're doing.

handling
stress

In all trouble you should seek God. You should not set him over against your troubles, but within them. God can only relieve your troubles if you in your anxiety cling to him. Trouble should not really be thought of as this thing or that in particular, for our whole life on earth involves trouble; and through the troubles of our earthly pilgrimage we find God.

Saint Augustine

a reminder

Before you dive into this study, spend a little time reviewing what you wrote in the previous lessons' Live sections. How are you doing? Check with your small-group members and review your progress toward the specified goals. If necessary, adjust your goals and plans and then recommit to them.

the defining line

Stress isn't just a part of work; it's a part of life. But a lot of the stress in our lives begins at work or comes from the need for work (more specifically, for the financial benefits of having a steady paycheck). As a result, work also provides a perfect place for learning how to respond to and handle stress.

Depending on your upbringing, personality, and background, stress may be easy or very challenging for you to handle. On a scale of one to ten (with ten being a lot), how much stress do you currently have in your life?

Using the same scale (this time with ten being very well), how do you think you're handling that stress?

Think back to a particularly stressful time in your life. How did you respond to the stress physically, emotionally, and spiritually? Is there anything you wish you would have done differently? Explain.

Consider sharing your responses with your group when you meet.

read Stressed Out

From "Stress Statistics" by Stress Directions, Inc.[1]

Stress is both additive and cumulative in its negative effects on individuals, organizations and societies.

Workplace stress continues to grow. In the U.S., experts at the Centers for Disease Control and the National Institute for Occupational Safety and Health are dedicated to studying stress. They've found:

- Stress is linked to physical and mental health, as well as decreased willingness to take on new and creative endeavors.
- Job burnout experienced by 25% to 40% of U.S. workers is blamed on stress.
- More than ever before, employee stress is being recognized as a major drain on corporate productivity and competitiveness.
- Depression, only one type of stress reaction, is predicted to be the leading occupational disease of the 21st century, responsible for more days lost than any other single factor.
- $300 billion, or $7,500 per employee, is spent annually in the U.S. on stress-related compensation claims, reduced productivity, absenteeism, health insurance costs, direct medical expenses (nearly 50% higher for workers who report stress), and employee turnover.

What's so different about today's workplace? Studies from organizations such as National Institutes for Occupational Safety and Health and the American Psychological Association show the following changes in working conditions have overburdened our traditional coping mechanisms:

- Growing psychological demands as we increase productivity demands and work longer hours
- The need to gather and apply growing amounts of information
- Job insecurity
- Demographic changes such as aging workers, female participation in the workforce, and the integration of a growing population of ethnic and racial minorities into the workplace
- The need for both men and women to balance obligations between work and family as women enter the workforce worldwide

---

first thoughts

like:

dislike:

agree:

disagree:

don't get it:

---

think

- Based on your personal experience, why do you think the level of stress at work continues to increase nationwide?
- What aspects of your job are stressful? How do you respond to the stress?
- Are you ever tempted to respond to stress with unhealthy patterns of behavior? If so, explain.
- How can you help coworkers become less stressed out?

pray

read Checking Your Stress Level

From "The Social Adjustment Rating Scale" by Thomas H. Holmes and Richard H. Rahe[2]

Life Event	Mean Value
Death of spouse	100
Divorce	73
Marital separation	65
Jail term	63
Death of close family member	63
Personal injury or illness	53
Marriage	50
Fired at work	47
Marital reconciliation	45
Retirement	45
Change in health of family member	44
Pregnancy	40
Sex difficulties	39
Gain of new family member	39
Business readjustment	39
Change in financial state	38
Death of close family friend	37
Change to different line of work	36
Change in number of arguments with spouse	35
Large mortgage	31
Foreclosure of mortgage or loan	30
Change in responsibilities of work	29
Son or daughter leaving home	29
Trouble with in-laws	29
Outstanding personal achievement	28
Spouse beginning or ending work	26
Beginning or ending school	26
Change in living conditions	25
Revision of personal habits	24

Trouble with boss	23
Change in work hours or conditions	20
Change in residence	20
Change in school	20
Change in recreation	19
Change in church activities	19
Change in social activities	18
Small mortgage or loan	17
Change in sleep habits	16
Change in the number of family get-togethers	15
Change in eating habits	15
Vacation	13
Christmas or other major holiday	12
Minor violations of the law	11

Underline each event that you have experienced in the last 12 months. Add up the total number of points associated with your experiences. (You can count events multiple times).

Each point represents a life change unit (LCU) or the amount of life stress a person encounters during a period of time. It's estimated that people who score more than 150 points may experience a decline in their health the following year. Those scoring between 150 to 300 carry a fifty percent chance of major illness, and those scoring 300 or more are 70 percent more likely to encounter a major life illness as a result of stress.

---

first thoughts

like:

dislike:

agree:

disagree:

don't get it:

---

think

- Compare your score to others' in your discussion group. Who has encountered the most life change in the last twelve months? Who has encountered the least?
- What is your response to the idea that stress can lead to illness? Do you agree or disagree? Why?
- How much of your stress, in life and work, is actually under your control? How much is beyond your control?
- Do you foresee your life increasing or decreasing in stress? What can you do to minimize your stress levels?

pray

read Paul's Journey

2 Corinthians 2:1-14

That's why I decided not to make another visit that could only be painful to both of us. If by merely showing up I would put you in an embarrassingly painful position, how would you then be free to cheer and refresh me?

That was my reason for writing a letter instead of coming—so I wouldn't have to spend a miserable time disappointing the very friends I had looked forward to cheering me up. I was convinced at the time I wrote it that what was best for me was also best for you. As it turned out, there was pain enough just in writing that letter, more tears than ink on the parchment. But I didn't write it to cause pain; I wrote it so you would know how much I care—oh, more than care—*love* you!

Now, regarding the one who started all this—the person in question who caused all this pain—I want you to know that I am not the one injured in this as much as, with a few exceptions, all of you. So I don't want to come down too hard. What the majority of you agreed to as punishment is punishment enough. Now is the time to forgive this man and help him back on his feet. If all you do is pour on the guilt, you could very well drown him in it. My counsel now is to pour on the love.

The focus of my letter wasn't on punishing the offender but on getting you to take responsibility for the health of the church. So if you forgive him, I forgive him. Don't think I'm carrying around a list of personal grudges. The fact is that I'm joining in with *your* forgiveness, as Christ is with us, guiding

first thoughts

like:

dislike:

agree:

disagree:

don't get it:

us. After all, we don't want to unwittingly give Satan an opening for yet more mischief—we're not oblivious to his sly ways!

When I arrived in Troas to proclaim the Message of the Messiah, I found the place wide open: God had opened the door; all I had to do was walk through it. But when I didn't find Titus waiting for me with news of your condition, I couldn't relax. Worried about you, I left and came on to Macedonia province looking for Titus and a reassuring word on you. And I got it, thank God!

think

- According to this passage, what was the source of Paul's stress?
- What does this passage reveal about the sources of your stress?
- In what situations do you find that you can't relax?
- How did Paul respond to his stress? Do you think he did the right thing? Why or why not? What would you have done differently?

pray

read The Money Margin

From "Not More Money, More Margin" by J. R. Rushik[3]

The leading cause of stress in a person's life is money. And even the number one reported problem in marriages is based on money. Everybody seems to need a little bit more. Not a lot more, but definitely more. Perhaps you've thought or spoken some of these statements: "If I could just get that raise, then I'll be all set . . ." "Just a few extra dollars each month and we'd be just fine . . ." "I'm not looking to be rich; I just need a little bit more to be comfortable . . ." Statements like these will cheat a person out of enjoying what they have. The problem is not how much money you take in; the problem is how much goes out.

Statistically, 80 percent of people state that they "need" to make a little more money. A person making $20,000 a year will say, "If I could only make $6,000 more, then my problems will be solved." While it's true that a person making 20k could probably use more money, the person making $30,000, $40,000 or $50,000 a year all seem to have the same request. Why? Because as a person's income increases, so does their lifestyle. More money, more expenses. The problem isn't the money—the problem is the margin.

Margin is that white space on the edge of a piece of paper. Margin is a few extra minutes in your busy schedule. And margin is the extra dollars in your budget. We need margin in every area of our lives. In fact, the amount of margin we have inversely determines the level of stress in our life. Think about it next time you leave your house at 12:20 p.m. for an appointment at 12:30 p.m. Everything should be fine. The drive is eight minutes long. You

first thoughts

like:

dislike:

agree:

disagree:

don't get it:

just finished your last project at 12:19 p.m., grabbed your stuff and hopped in the car. No problem. This is a normal routine for most of us. Well, what happens when there is construction or an accident on your intended route? Your margin begins to decrease from three minutes to two minutes, until you don't have any margin left. As your margin of time gets smaller and smaller, your stress level will get higher and higher. If you had 10 minutes of margin there would be no stress, no problem. Margin makes the difference.

think

- How much margin do you have in your life?
- Do you tend to allow more margin in your finances, schedule, or relationships? In what areas of your life do you tend to cut it close?
- Do you think having a wider margin in your life would affect your stress level? Why or why not?
- What can you do to create wider margins in your life?

pray

read God Worship

Matthew 6:25-34

"If you decide for God, living a life of God-worship, it follows that you don't fuss about what's on the table at mealtimes or whether the clothes in your closet are in fashion. There is far more to your life than the food you put in your stomach, more to your outer appearance than the clothes you hang on your body. Look at the birds, free and unfettered, not tied down to a job description, careless in the care of God. And you count far more to him than birds.

"Has anyone by fussing in front of the mirror ever gotten taller by so much as an inch? All this time and money wasted on fashion—do you think it makes that much difference? Instead of looking at the fashions, walk out into the fields and look at the wildflowers. They never primp or shop, but have you ever seen color and design quite like it? The ten best-dressed men and women in the country look shabby alongside them.

"If God gives such attention to the appearance of wildflowers—most of which are never even seen—don't you think he'll attend to you, take pride in you, do his best for you? What I'm trying to do here is to get you to relax, to not be so preoccupied with *getting*, so you can respond to God's *giving*. People who don't know God and the way he works fuss over these things, but you know both God and how he works. Steep your life in God-reality, God-initiative, God-provisions. Don't worry about missing out. You'll find all your everyday human concerns will be met.

first thoughts
like:
dislike:
agree:
disagree:
don't get it:

"Give your entire attention to what God is doing right now, and don't get worked up about what may or may not happen tomorrow. God will help you deal with whatever hard things come up when the time comes."

think

- In what areas of your life are you most tempted to "fuss"?
- In what types of situations are you tempted to worry that you're "missing out"? Do you think this adds stress to your life? Why or why not?
- What does stress reveal about your faith and trust in God? What prevents you from trusting Him more with all the details of your life?

pray

live   The Redefining

Take a few moments to skim through the notes you've made in these readings. What do they reveal about the way you handle stress? Based on what you've read and discussed, is there anything you want to change?

What, if anything, is stopping you from making this change?

Do you have any baggage or unhealthy behavior patterns that tend to create stress in your life? Make a list. Share at least one of them with the members of your group.

How much pressure do you put on yourself to do too much? What is the result of this excess pressure or lack of pressure? What can you do to develop and maintain healthy expectations regarding yourself, your life, and your work?

Talk with a close friend about all of the above. Brainstorm together about what it might take to move toward God in this area of your life. Determine what this looks like in a practical sense and then list any measurable goals you want to shoot for here. Review these goals each week to see how you're doing.

balancing
work
and life

"Are you tired? Worn out? Burned out on religion?
Come to me. Get away with me and you'll recover
your life. I'll show you how to take a real rest.
Walk with me and work with me—watch how I do it.
Learn the unforced rhythms of grace. I won't lay
anything heavy or ill-fitting on you. Keep company with me and you'll learn to live freely and
lightly."

Matthew 11:28-30

a reminder

*Before you dive into this study, spend a little time reviewing what
you wrote in the previous lessons' Live sections. How are you doing?
Check with your small-group members and review your progress
toward the specified goals. If necessary, adjust your goals and plans
and then recommit to them.*

the defining line

Whether you realize it or not, there is a rhythm to your life. Your life may be
more like rock, ska, emo, pop, country, or classical—but regardless of what
it is, when you combine your actions and activities into one "song," you'll
find there's a certain rhythm. You may be more prone to a fast, intense, or
upbeat rhythm, or you may find that your life has a slower, more relaxed

rhythm. Either way, when you live a healthy, vibrant life, you can't help but emit a beautiful song.

But what happens when things get out of whack? What happens when you're living life too fast, too hard, or not at all? What happens to the rhythms of your life then?

What does your life song sound like right now?

A healthy sense of balance in your life doesn't just help hold your schedule together—it helps hold you together. As a practical exercise, have everyone in your discussion group stand on one foot for as long as possible. Who lasted the longest? In the space below, describe your experience in a few sentences.

What did you have to do physically and mentally to maintain your balance? What caused you to lose your balance?

In what ways do you feel unbalanced in your life right now? In what ways is your job contributing to your lack of balance? What can you do to regain a sense of balance in your life?

Consider sharing your responses with your group when you meet.

read Speed of Life

from "My Life as a Fast-Paced Junkie" by Joe Riggio[1]

I sometimes sit in traffic wondering why in the world we are not moving faster. It is a green light, and traffic should be moving! I am convinced it is caused by one driver who is just not moving . . . well . . . faster. I mean, don't they know I am on the fast track in life here? I am in the fast lane, driving my fast car, making fast money and on my way to get some fast food. If that person plugging up the fast lane wants to do some Sunday driving, then maybe they should move out of the fast lane. Or maybe I am just moving too fast and missing some significant point in life.

As a twentysomething, I have been on this fast track ever since I was in college. I tried moving, doing, eating, driving, making and being faster with success. I got into a fast-paced career with lots of success, at least monetarily speaking—401(k), benefits, opportunities, contacts and so forth. I had more money in my fast-pace life, which was a big reason I got in the fast lane. With more money, I got to spend more time at Best Buy, Amazon. com, Barnes & Noble and my favorite Starbucks. I mean, who was going to complain? Not me.

There was never a class, at least not at my university, which spoke of balance and being present in the moment. I saw some books on the matter, but I was more interested in books that helped me make money faster or how to do "this or that" faster. To me, those two things—balance and being present—were foreign. I guess you could say I picked up a lot of my fast-paced antics through society, culture, experiences and just being a normal American. I learned quickly how the world in the fast lane would give me things, well, at least tangible things. Everyone around me bought into this lifestyle. The keep-up-or-get-left-behind mentality. Move it or lose it. I told myself I was not going to lose anything.

I would try to squeeze an extra hour into my day. I would try to do my job faster and better than the others. I would try to talk faster to get my point across quicker. I would try to get someplace earlier so I didn't "miss out"—my entire life was on this treadmill. If you have never experienced this, I have an exercise for you to try. Get on a treadmill and crank it up to its top speed. Set the time limit for five minutes and run as fast as you can. At first you will notice your endorphins buzzing and you will be feeling good, *but then* you get tunnel vision, your breathing will become labored, perspiration will rise, muscles fatigue quicker, and it becomes less than enjoyable. The point is, while on the treadmill you have quick, immediate results, like getting to your destination or goal faster, but the journey or experience overall can be taxing. This is how I felt.

What I have learned is how important the gift of now is. God, I believe, is more concerned about you and living fully in the present than concentrating solely on what our plans are in the next five years. I look back and wonder how many "aha" moments, lessons to be learned, meaningful conversations I missed. I was just moving through life at a blistering speed while acquiring new things and conquering new territories. I was never really satisfied. I was always half empty, and I did not just have one glass to fill but several. I always had this void and empty feeling in the pit of my soul, but nobody really knew it because I was either moving too fast for them to notice or I myself was never really aware of it.

I was never one to go to church: I didn't have time and never really felt close to God. He couldn't keep up with me, I would tell myself. Religion and my relationship with God did not fit into my schedule. I finally told myself I had to be still, attend Sunday church, read the Bible and just be. God is amazing. He constantly was aware of me and was never too busy to forget about me. He never gave up on me, and when I was ready, He revealed Himself to my eyes and soul.

What changed me was slowing down my life. At first it was just a little bit at a time, but I noticed as I slowed down, my conversations and experiences with God became more meaningful and more heartfelt. I was learning how to speak to God in the midst of all this craziness I created in my life. I was learning that busyness does not equal a more fulfilled life. My relationship with God was more fulfilling than money, a car or my fast-lane career. He wanted me to *experience* life and to take my time and not necessarily blow through life. I think this is somewhat counter cultural because in today's world the term "fast" is considered convenient. But sometimes convenience comes with a price, like quality. Quality time with God and yourself, two of the most important people you should get to know.

With the help and patience of my church community, my wife and my family, I am learning that we must all know that God loves us *no matter what* and there is *nothing* that can separate us from His love. He does not care about our income, our job, our DVD collections, our latest gadgets or our wardrobe. He cares about you and me as His sons and daughters. Also, I have learned one of the most important things God has given us is time. Take time to live in the present and *you will be* taken care of. Slow down in your life and take time for yourself. When you take time and you live in the present, I can almost guarantee you will experience a more fulfilling and enriching life than if you were to breeze through the day, month, year and your life. After all, it took God a few days—not one—to create the world. If God can take His time, then I suggest you can too.

---

first thoughts

like:

dislike:

agree:

disagree:

don't get it:

---

think

- Rate your life with a speed between 0 and 100 mph. Do you wish you were moving faster or slower? What prevents you from changing the pace of your life? At what speed do you think Jesus lived His life?

- How does living a fast-paced life affect your job? Your relationships? Your health?
- How does living a high-speed life affect your relationship with God? Are you able to connect with God better when you slow down or speed up? Why?

pray

ead Storms

Matthew 7:24-29

These words I speak to you are not incidental additions to your life, home-owner improvements to your standard of living. They are foundational words, words to build a life on. If you work these words into your life, you are like a smart carpenter who built his house on solid rock. Rain poured down, the river flooded, a tornado hit—but nothing moved that house. It was fixed to the rock.

"But if you just use my words in Bible studies and don't work them into your life, you are like a stupid carpenter who built his house on the sandy beach. When a storm rolled in and the waves came up, it collapsed like a house of cards."

When Jesus concluded his address, the crowd burst into applause. They had never heard teaching like this. It was apparent that he was living everything he was saying—quite a contrast to their religion teachers! This was the best teaching they had ever heard.

---

first thoughts

like:

dislike:

agree:

disagree:

don't get it:

---

think

- Why do you think balance is such an important issue? In what situations do you think the balance or lack of balance in someone's life is made evident?
- Do you think it's possible for people to create their own "storms"? Have you ever created a storm in your life? If so, explain.
- In order to live a balanced life, how important is having a solid foundation? What are you doing to ensure that your life is built on a solid foundation?

pray

ead Finding Strength

Isaiah 40:27-31

Why would you ever complain, O Jacob,
　　or, whine, Israel, saying,
"GOD has lost track of me.
　　He doesn't care what happens to me"?
Don't you know anything? Haven't you been listening?
GOD doesn't come and go. God *lasts*.
　　He's Creator of all you can see or imagine.
He doesn't get tired out, doesn't pause to catch his breath.
　　And he knows *everything*, inside and out.
He energizes those who get tired,
　　gives fresh strength to dropouts.
For even young people tire and drop out,
　　young folk in their prime stumble and fall.
But those who wait upon GOD get fresh strength.
　　They spread their wings and soar like eagles,
They run and don't get tired,
　　they walk and don't lag behind.

first thoughts

like:

dislike:

agree:

disagree:

don't get it:

think

- What does this passage reveal about balance? Is anyone immune from doing too much?
- Have you ever been in a tough job situation? Where did you find God in your situation?
- Do you ever struggle with complaining about your job? What can you do to reduce the amount of complaining you do?
- To whom should you go when you are weak? What stops you from turning to God in those situations?

pray

ead Impossible to Balance

rom "Balance? Schmalance!" by Martha Beck[2]

t's five o'clock in the morning. I've been awake for about 23 hours, having truggled vainly to fit in writing between yesterday's tasks: getting the car ixed, taking the dog to the vet, answering e-mail, going grocery shopping, riving my kids to music lessons, seeing clients, picking up deli sandwiches or dinner and cuddling a 12-year-old through some of the horrors of uberty. I finally sat down at my computer around midnight—and looked p just now to see the sun rising.

Understand three things: (1) I don't have a job. I freelance, which means procrastinate and get away with it; (2) my children are not young. They valk, talk, bathe, diagnose their own viruses; and (3) I'm kind of supposed o be an expert at combining career and family. I conducted years of socio- ogical research on the topic, wrote a big fat book about it. Plus, I'm a life oach. You'd think I could live a balanced life as a 21st-century American voman.

Ha. In fact, having done all that research, I can tell you with absolute issurance that it is impossible for women to achieve the kind of balance ecommended by many well-meaning self-help counselors. I didn't say such palance is difficult to attain. I didn't say it's rare. I said it's *impossible*. Our :ulture's definition of what women should be is fundamentally, irreconcilably unbalanced. That's the bad news. The good news is that the very imbalance of our culture is forcing women to find equilibrium in an entirely new way.

The joy of being unbalanced

If someone condemned you because, say, you failed to prevent Hurricane Andrew, you wouldn't dissolve in shame or work to overcome your inadequacy. You'd probably conclude that your critic was nuts, then simply dismiss the whole issue. That's the wonderful thing about seeing that our society makes impossible demands on all women. You free yourself to ignore social pressures and begin creating a life that comes from your own deepest desires, hopes and dreams. You'll stop living life from the outside in and begin living it from the inside out.

Women describe the moments when they really "got" that th expectations they'd been trying to fulfill were unfulfillable. They say, thi epiphany was terrible, because it meant relinquishing the goal of tot social acceptance. But it was also the beginning of freedom, of learnin to seek guidance by turning inward to the heart, rather than outward t social prescriptions.

If you feel trapped by contradictory demands, you may want to joi this gentle rebellion. You can help create a new cultural paradigm, one tha replaces conformity with honesty, convention with creativity, and judgmer with kindness. That, in the end, is the gift of the disequilibrium that societ has bequeathed to all of us. Being forced to seek balance within ourselve we can make our unsteady, stumbling days feel less and less like disaste and more and more like a joyful dance—the dance of a wildly, wonderfull perfectly unbalanced life.

---

first thoughts

like:

dislike:

agree:

disagree:

don't get it:

---

think

- In what ways do you think our society paints an unrealistic picture of productivity?
- What expectations do you place on yourself that sometimes throw you out of balance?
- What stops you from letting go of those expectations?
- What does a healthy, balanced lifestyle look like for you?

pray

read Balancing the Checkbook

1 Timothy 6:3-10

If you have leaders there who teach otherwise, who refuse the solid words o
our Master Jesus and this godly instruction, tag them for what they are: ignoran
windbags who infect the air with germs of envy, controversy, bad-mouthing
suspicious rumors. Eventually there's an epidemic of backstabbing, and truth i
but a distant memory. They think religion is a way to make a fast buck.

A devout life does bring wealth, but it's the rich simplicity of being your
self before God. Since we entered the world penniless and will leave it penni
less, if we have bread on the table and shoes on our feet, that's enough.

But if it's only money these leaders are after, they'll self-destruct in n
time. Lust for money brings trouble and nothing but trouble. Going dow
that path, some lose their footing in the faith completely and live to regre
it bitterly ever after.

---

first thoughts

like:

dislike:

agree:

disagree:

don't get it:

---

think

- In what areas of your life do you struggle with contentment? When are you the most content? What prevents you from being more content?
- Have there been times when you've worn yourself out or over-worked yourself in order to afford more luxuries?
- Write a paragraph that answers this question: How much is enough?
- What steps can you take to develop a balanced view of money and material wealth?
- What can you do to be more generous with your time, money, and other resources?

pray

live   The Redefining

Take a few moments to skim through the notes you've made in these readings. What do they tell you about how balanced your life is? Based on what you've read and discussed, is there anything you want to change?

What, if anything, is stopping you from making this change?

How is lack of balance an inhibitor in your life? Is there anything that's preventing you from regaining balance right now?

Make a list of the effects an unbalanced life has on your physical, emotional, spiritual, and overall well-being. Where do you "take the biggest hit" when you're out of balance? Share your list with the members of your small group.

Talk with a close friend about all of the above. Brainstorm together about what it might take to move toward God in this area of your life. Determine what this looks like in a practical sense and then list any measurable goals you want to shoot for here. Review these goals each week to see how you're doing.

faith and
the
workplace

Through thick and thin, keep your hearts at attention, in adoration before Christ, your Master. Be ready to speak up and tell anyone who asks why you're living the way you are, and always with the utmost courtesy.

1 Peter 3:15

a reminder

Before you dive into this study, spend a little time reviewing what you wrote in the previous lessons' Live sections. How are you doing? Check with your small-group members and review your progress toward the specified goals. If necessary, adjust your goals and plans and then recommit to them.

the defining line

Depending on where you work, it may be easy to check your faith at the door. It may be inappropriate or even illegal for you to discuss religious issues at work. You may find yourself in a workplace where people discourage or are even hostile toward talking about spiritual issues. Yet even in these situations, you were designed to reflect Christlikeness.

Think about your workplace. In what ways is it easy to share your faith? In what ways is it challenging?

What stops you from talking more about your faith at work?

In what ways can you actively preach the gospel at work *without using words*?

In what situations are you tempted to be more right than righteous?

Consider sharing your responses with your group when you meet.

read The God of Everywhere

From *Praise Habit: Finding God in Sunsets and Sushi* by David Crowder[1]

I used to think I knew where to find God. He seemed to always be where I put Him last.

He was in Sunday school every Sunday morning. He was in "big church" right after. He was there most Sunday nights, too. He was around our dinner table when my father read from the blue Bible-story books. He was there when I prayed before meals. He was there most times I prayed elsewhere, too. He was there during my quiet times. He was at church on Wednesday nights. He was *really* there at summer camp. He loved church camp. I think He just liked summers better in general. Once school started back, the moments with Him were farther spaced, it seems. I enjoyed finding Him. It felt like things were right. Even if they weren't, it felt okay. I wanted more moments with Him. I heard there was a Bible study on Monday nights, so I went, and sure enough—He was there. I had an accountability group and we met on Tuesdays, and sure enough—He was there, too. I heard about another Bible study that met on Thursdays, so I went, and wouldn't you know it, there He was. He began showing up in the songs we sang around 1983. It was called contemporary worship. It was great. He was always in these songs, so I would sing them whenever I wanted to find Him, and sure enough—there He'd be. By the time I got to college I thought I had it all sorted out with everything in its place. Then tragedy came.

Tragedy always comes. If it hasn't come for you, it will. Not the losing-your-homework kind or the having-to-flush-your-goldfish kind, but the kind that leaves you stripped. The kind that tears from you all the ideas about living you once believed untearable. Mine came my junior year of college, and it came in a phone call. It was my mom. She said, "David, something very terrible has happened." The words that followed were bombs. As they came hurtling toward me through miles of telephone wire, my muscles turned liquid, and when she finished, I was left wilted on the floor, and God was not there. At least I could no longer find Him. And I had no idea where to begin looking again. The places I used to frequent, I no longer trusted. In seven minutes everything I had thought about everything was dramatically different. . . .

There was a lot of sorting out to be done concerning most things and where they were to be placed in this faith I carried or that was carrying me, and it was proving to be a daunting task. And then in the middle of this sorting, an explosion. I was covered in shrapnel, clotlessly bleeding. And when I had bled out, when there was nothing left, I found Him. And He was not where I thought He was. Nor where I had put Him last.

He was in a Chick-fil-A sandwich.

I have loved Chick-fil-A my whole life. But when your world implodes, nothing tastes good. I was poking at the thing and a thought hit me that there is one part of the sandwich I don't enjoy. There is about a quarter of the breast that consistently dissolves into a lesser grade of meat and soggy breading. I pulled the top bun off and tore the portion away that didn't look appealing. There was a natural break in the meat. It was easily separated. I put the top back on and ate. It was the best chicken sandwich I had ever eaten. I wadded up the foil sandwich bag and smiled for the first time in a really long while.

It may not sound like a real breakthrough, but for me it was truly cathartic. In a small, decisive moment I was aware of what was *good* and took effort to peel away what wasn't and in the process became re-enamored with the Giver of good. I remembered our beginnings, when that statement "It was good" was first uttered. I thought about how the *bad* was never intended. Things started to come to life. Blood that had slowed to a crawl began to find its way through my veins again.

The consequences of this discovery were huge. If He was in a sandwich, where else could He be found? Every moment was becoming holy. Nothing was nonspiritual. This was habitual praise—a perpetually sacred acknowledgment of the Giver of every good thing. A

first thoughts

like:

dislike:

agree:

disagree:

don't get it:

relentless embracing of good and a discarding of bad with an awareness of the one who in the beginning spoke those life-affirming words.

When good is found and we embrace it with abandon, we embrace the Giver of it. . . . This is the Praise Habit. Finding God moment by revelatory moment, in the sacred and the mundane, in the valley and on the hill, in triumph and tragedy, and living praise erupting because of it. This is what we were made for.

think

- In what ways do you practice "the Praise Habit" in everyday life? In what ways do you practice it at work?
- Do you think you need to work for a Christian company to have a Christian experience at work? Why or why not?
- Describe a moment when you were able to recognize God at work. What made the experience so special?
- What stops you from having more "Praise Habit" moments at work?
- What steps can you take to become more aware of God in your job?

pray

read Hands and Feet

1 Corinthians 12:13-31

By means of his one Spirit, we all said good-bye to our partial and piece-meal lives. We each used to independently call our own shots, but then we entered into a large and integrated life in which *he* has the final say in everything. (This is what we proclaimed in word and action when we were baptized.) Each of us is now a part of his resurrection body, refreshed and sustained at one fountain—his Spirit—where we all come to drink. The old labels we once used to identify ourselves—labels like Jew or Greek, slave or free—are no longer useful. We need something larger, more comprehensive.

I want you to think about how all this makes you more significant, not less. A body isn't just a single part blown up into something huge. It's all the different-but-similar parts arranged and functioning together. If Foot said, "I'm not elegant like Hand, embellished with rings; I guess I don't belong to this body," would that make it so? If Ear said, "I'm not beautiful like Eye, limpid and expressive; I don't deserve a place on the head," would you want to remove it from the body? If the body was all eye, how could it hear? If all ear, how could it smell? As it is, we see that God has carefully placed each part of the body right where he wanted it.

But I also want you to think about how this keeps your significance from getting blown up into self-importance. For no matter how significant you are, it is only because of what you are a *part* of. An enormous eye or a gigantic hand wouldn't be a body, but a monster. What we have is one body with many parts, each its proper size and in its proper place. No part is important on its own. Can you imagine Eye telling Hand, "Get lost; I don't need you"? Or, Head telling Foot, "You're fired; your job has been phased out"? As a matter of fact, in practice it works the other way—the "lower" the part, the more basic, and therefore necessary. You can live without an eye, for instance, but not without a stomach. When it's a part of your own body you are concerned with, it makes *no* difference whether the part is visible or clothed, higher or lower. You give it dignity and honor just as it is, without comparisons. If anything, you have more concern for the lower parts than the higher. If you had to choose, wouldn't you prefer good digestion to full-bodied hair?

The way God designed our bodies is a model for understanding our lives together as a church: every part dependent on every other part, the parts we mention and the parts we don't, the parts we see and the parts we don't. If one part hurts, every other part is involved in the hurt, and in the healing. If one part flourishes, every other part enters into the exuberance.

You are Christ's body—that's who you are! You must never forget this. Only as you accept your part of that body does your "part" mean anything. You're familiar with some of the parts that God has formed in his church, which is his "body":

apostles
prophets
teachers
miracle workers
healers
helpers
organizers
those who pray in tongues.

---

first thoughts

like:

dislike:

agree:

disagree:

don't get it:

But it's obvious by now, isn't it, that Christ's church is a complete Body and not a gigantic, unidimensional Part? It's not all Apostle, not all Prophet, not all Miracle Worker, not all Healer, not all Prayer in Tongues, not all Interpreter of Tongues. And yet some of you keep competing for so-called "important" parts.

But now I want to lay out a far better way for you.

think

- How do you think the church is supposed to interact with the world? What stops the church from interacting this way? What stops you from interacting this way?
- As part of Christ's body, how are you being the hands and feet of Christ to those in your workplace? What stops you from reaching out and serving more?
- What one-of-a-kind opportunities does your job offer for you to be Jesus to people who would otherwise not attend church or read the Bible? In what ways are you taking advantage of those opportunities?

pray

read The Importance of Discipline

From *Celebration of Discipline: The Path to Spiritual Growth* by Richard J. Foster[2]

Superficiality is the curse of our age. The doctrine of instant satisfaction is a primary spiritual problem. The desperate need today is not for a greater number of intelligent people, or gifted people, but for deep people.

The classical Disciplines of the spiritual life [meditation, prayer, fasting, study, simplicity, solitude, submission, service, confession, worship, guidance, and celebration] call us to move beyond surface living into the depths. They invite us to explore the inner caverns of the spiritual realm. They urge us to be the answer to a hollow world. . . .

We must not be led to believe that the Disciplines are only for spiritual giants and hence beyond our reach, or only for contemplatives who devote all their time to prayer and meditation. Far from it. God intends the Disciplines of the spiritual life to be for ordinary human beings: people who have jobs, who care for children, who wash dishes and mow lawns. In fact, the Disciplines are best exercised in the midst of our relationships with our husband or wife, our brothers and sisters, our friends and neighbors.

---

first thoughts

like:

dislike:

agree:

disagree:

don't get it:

Neither should we think of the Spiritual Disciplines as some dull drudgery aimed at exterminating laughter from the face of the earth. Joy is the keynote of all the Disciplines. The purpose of the Disciplines is liberation from the stifling slavery to self-interest and fear. When the inner spirit is liberated from all that weighs it down, it can hardly be described as dull drudgery. Singing, dancing, even shouting characterize the Disciplines of the spiritual life.

think

- Which spiritual disciplines do you practice on a regular basis? Which do you tend to neglect?
- How important are spiritual disciplines to your faith journey? What impact have they had on you personally?
- Respond to this statement: "The Disciplines are best exercised in the midst of our normal daily activities." In what ways do you practice spiritual disciplines at work? In what ways could you practice them at work? What would it take for you to begin practicing them?

pray

read Faith at Work

From "The Faith at Work Movement: Opening 'The 9 to 5 Window'" by Os Hillman[3]

Pat Rainey is arriving at work today at 7 a.m. It's not because her administrative assistant position requires her to do so. It's because she's part of a handful of women and men who regularly meet to pray for the company. They've been doing this for more a year now, believing that this is an assignment God has given them.

And they have been encouraged to see how their prayer is impacting the company. Over the last twelve months Pat has seen at least twelve people come to Christ in her 225 employee insurance company in Atlanta. She has seen people get physically healed in meetings and she has seen God confirm key corporate decisions. In short, she has seen the supernatural: the Lord is moving in her company.

As you probably know, for years Christians have sought to evangelize a largely unreached people in what is called "The 10/40 Window"—the area of land between the 10th and 40th parallel north of the Equator, spanning from Africa through east Asia. But what you might not know is that there's another window that's opening to allow Christians to introduce people to God: "The 9 to 5 Window." And it's a window of opportunity that's just as exciting.

You see, Pat Rainey's story is not just an Atlanta story. It's a story that's being recounted in hundreds of organizations around the globe this very day. Quietly but persistently, God is revealing Himself to the world through the workplace.

An overview of the faith at work movement

In November 1999, *Business Week* magazine noted that "five years ago, only one conference on spirituality and the workplace could be identified; now there are hundreds. There are more than 10,000 Bible and prayer groups in workplaces that meet regularly." Two years later, *Fortune* magazine confirmed the existence of a movement in a cover story on "God & Business," reporting the marketplace presence of "a mostly unorganized mass of believers—a counterculture bubbling up all over corporate America—who want to bridge the traditional divide between spirituality and work." The article went on to say: "Historically, such folk operated below the radar, on their own or in small workplace groups where they prayed or studied the Bible. But now they are getting organized and going public to agitate for change. People who want to mix God and business are rebels on several fronts. They reject the centuries-old American conviction that spirituality is a private matter. They challenge religious thinkers who disdain business as an inherently impure pursuit. They disagree with business people who say that religion is unavoidably divisive."

In the wake of these articles, the Christian media has also highlighted the movement, with stories appearing in *New Man*, *Charisma*, *Christianity Today*, and *Decision* magazine. Christian leaders, too, are acknowledging the trend. "I believe one of the next great moves of God is going to be through the believers in the workplace," said Billy Graham. His son Franklin put it in the present tense: "God has begun an evangelism movement in the workplace that has the potential to transform our society as we know it." And Henry Blackaby (author of *Experiencing God*), who meets regularly with CEOs of Fortune 500 companies to discuss what it means to bring Christ into a corporate environment, observes: "I've never seen the activity of God this deeply in the business community as I do right now."

Kent Humphreys, a businessman and the president of Fellowship of Companies for Christ, a ministry devoted to serving executives and CEOs, wholeheartedly agrees with such assessments: "Leaders in the workplace from every part of the country are experiencing a hunger to be involved and they're searching the web to find those who are of like heart. Those who are a little further along in the movement understand the principle, but are now more anxious for training and practical helps of what it looks like in their workplace."

And the movement is not just an American phenomenon. Brenda deCharmoy, a business consultant from South Africa, remarks: "I am beginning to see more and more people and churches becoming aware that the workplace is a key area for God, and we should give it more attention. I think the tide has built quite a lot this last year. There is more questioning by workplace people of the issue of God in their 9 to 5 time. I also see more leaders realizing that going to church and then leaving God behind does not work in the end."

Surely it does not, and people in myriad places are appreciating that daily. In fact, in 1998 I began writing a daily email devotional called *TGIF, Today God Is First*. It has now grown to more than 70,000 subscribers. What I have learned from the feedback to my devotional is that people are hungry to know how to effectively integrate their faith life with their work life, and they are energized by the call. One subscriber summed up well what God is doing through *TGIF*: "I never really considered my secular work as a ministry until I read your (devotional). . . . Now I feel I have as much a ministry as my pastor. I simply have a different mission field."

---

first thoughts

like:

dislike:

agree:

disagree:

don't get it:

---

think

- What do you think of the Faith at Work movement? Why do you think so many believers check their faith at the door of their workplace?
- Do you think that to be involved in ministry you need to work at a church or an official Christian organization? Why or why not?
- In addition to your job, what other areas of your life can be an opportunity to express and live out your faith? Are there any areas you've neglected or overlooked?

- Respond to Billy Graham's statement: "I believe one of the next great moves of God is going to be through the believers in the workplace." What can you do to become a part of that movement?

pray

read Why You're Here

Matthew 5:13-16

"Let me tell you why you are here. You're here to be salt-seasoning that brings out the God-flavors of this earth. If you lose your saltiness, how will people taste godliness? You've lost your usefulness and will end up in the garbage.

"Here's another way to put it: You're here to be light, bringing out the God-colors in the world. God is not a secret to be kept. We're going public with this, as public as a city on a hill. If I make you light-bearers, you don't think I'm going to hide you under a bucket, do you? I'm putting you on a light stand. Now that I've put you there on a hilltop, on a light stand—shine! Keep open house; be generous with your lives. By opening up to others, you'll prompt people to open up with God, this generous Father in heaven."

---

first thoughts

like:

dislike:

agree:

disagree:

don't get it:

---

think

- In what ways are you being "salt-seasoning" at your workplace? In what ways are you bringing out the "God-flavors"?

- What do you think it means when the passage says, "You've los[t] your usefulness and will end up in the garbage"?
- What tempts you to lose your saltiness at work?
- What can you do to lead a more generous life at work?

pray

live   The Redefining

Take a few moments to skim through the notes you've made in these readings. What do they tell you about living the God-infused life at work? Based on what you've read and discussed, is there anything you want to change?

What, if anything, is stopping you from making this change?

How often do you look for the sacred in your workplace? What can you do to become more aware of God's presence in every aspect of your life?

Is there anything in your life—compromise, sin, doubt, anger—that is preventing you from reflecting God at your workplace? If so, spend some time this week talking to God about this.

Talk with a close friend about all of the above. Brainstorm together about what it might take to move toward God in this area of your life. Determine what this looks like in a practical sense and then list any measurable goals you want to shoot for here.

Even though you've reached the end of this discussion guide, progress toward a better understanding of your role in the workplace should continue. Commit to discussing your goals and discoveries with small-group members or friends as you attempt to live a God-infused life every day.

discussion group
study tips

After going through the study on your own, it's time to sit down with others and go deeper. A group of eight to ten is optimal, but smaller groups will allow members to participate more.

Here are a few thoughts on how to make the most of your group discussion time.

Set ground rules. You don't need many. Here are two:

First, you'll want group members to make a commitment to the entire eight-week study. A binding legal document with notarized signatures and commitments written in blood probably isn't necessary—but *you* know your friends best. Just remember this: Significant personal growth happens when group members spend enough time together to really get to know each other. Hit-and-miss attendance rarely allows this to occur.

Second, agree together that everyone's story is important. Time is a valuable commodity, so if you have only an hour to spend together, do your best to give each person ample time to express concerns, pass along insights, and generally feel like a participating member of the group. Small-group discussions are not monologues.

Meet regularly. Choose a time and place and stick to it. No one likes showing up to a restaurant at noon, only to discover that the meeting was moved to seven in the evening at so-and-so's house. Consistency removes stress that could otherwise frustrate discussion and subsequent personal growth. It's only eight weeks. You can do this.

Think ahead. Whoever is leading or organizing the study needs to keep an eye on the calendar. No matter what day or time you pick, you're probably going to run into a date that just doesn't work for people. Maybe it's a holiday. Maybe there's a huge concert or conference in town. Maybe there's a random week when everyone is going to be out of town. Keep in communication with each other about the meetings and be flexible if you do have to reschedule a meeting or skip a week.

Talk openly. If you enter this study with shields up, you're probably not alone. And you're not a "bad person" for your hesitation to unpack your life in front of friends or strangers. Maybe you're skeptical about the value of revealing the deepest parts of who you are to others. Maybe you're simply too afraid of what might fall out of the suitcase. You don't have to go to a place where you're uncomfortable. If you want to sit and listen, offer a few thoughts, or even express a surface level of your own pain, go ahead. But don't neglect what brings you to this place—that desperation. You can't ignore it away. Dip your feet in the water of brutally honest discussion and you may choose to dive in. There is healing here.

Stay on task. Be wary of sharing material that falls into the Too Much Information (TMI) category. Don't spill unnecessary stuff. This is about discovering how *you* can be a better person.

Hold each other accountable. The Live section is an important gear in the "redefinition" machine. If you're really ready for positive change—for spiritual growth—you'll want to take this section seriously. Get personal when you summarize your discoveries. Be practical as you compose your goals. And make sure you're realistic as you determine a plan for accountability. Be extraordinarily loving but brutally honest as you examine each other's Live sections. The stuff on this page must be doable. Don't hold back—this is where the rubber meets the road.

frequently
asked
questions

'm stuck. I've read the words on the page, but they just don't connect. Am I missing something?

Be patient. There's no need for speed-reading. Reread the words. Pray about them. Reflect on the questions at the bottom of the page. Consider rewriting the reading in a way that makes sense to you. Meditate on one idea at a time. Read Scripture passages in different Bible translations. Ask a friend for help. Skip the section and come back to it later. And don't beat yourself up if you still don't connect. Turn the page and keep seeking.

This study includes a wide variety of readings. Some are intended to provoke. Others are intended to subdue. Some are meant to apply to a thinker, others to a feeler, and still others to an experiential learner. If your groove is pop culture, science, relationships, art, or something completely different, there's something in here that you're naturally going to click with, but that doesn't mean that you should just brush off the rest of the readings. It means that in those no-instant-click moments, you're going to have to broaden your perspective and think outside your own box. You may be surprised by what you discover.

One or two people in our small group tend to dominate the discussion. Is there any polite way of handling this?

Did you set up ground rules with your group? If not, review the suggestions in the previous section and incorporate them. Then do this: Before each discussion, remind participants that each person's thoughts, insights, concerns, and opinions are important. Note the time you have for you meeting and then dive in.

If this still doesn't help, you may need to speak to the person who ha arm-wrestled control. Do so in a loving manner, expressing your since concern for what the person is talking about and inviting others to weigh i as well. Please note: A one-person-dominated discussion isn't *always* a ba thing. Your role in a small group is not only to explore and expand you own understanding; it's also to support one another. If someone truly need more of the floor, give it to him. There will be times when the needs of th one outweigh the needs of the many. Use good judgment and allow extr space when needed. Your time might be next week.

One or two people in our small group rarely say anything. How shoul we handle this?

Recognize that not everyone will be comfortable sharing. Depending o her background, personality, and comfort level, an individual may rarel say anything at all. There are two things to remember. First, love a per son right where she is. This may be one of her first experiences as par of a Bible discussion group. She may be feeling insecure because sh doesn't know the Bible as well as other members of the group. She ma just be shy or introverted. She may still be sorting out what she believe Whatever the case, make her feel welcome and loved. Thank her for com ing, and if she misses a meeting, call to check up on her. After one of th studies, you may want to ask her what she thought about the discussio And after a few meetings, you can try to involve her in the discussion b asking everyone in the group to respond to a certain question. Just mak sure the question you ask doesn't put anyone on the spot.

During our meeting time, we find ourselves spending so much tim catching up with each other—what happened over the previous week—tha we don't have enough time for the actual study.

If the friendships within your group grow tight, you may need t establish some time just to hang out and catch up with one another. Thi is a healthy part of a successful discussion group. You can do this befor or after the actual study group time. Some groups prefer to share a mea together before the study, and other groups prefer to stay afterward an munch on snacks. Whatever your group chooses, it's important to have established start and finish times for your group members. That way, the people who are on a tight schedule can know when to show up to catch the main part of the meeting.

At our meetings, there are times when one or two people will become really vulnerable about something they're struggling with or facing. It's an awkward thing for our group to try to handle. What should we do?

This study is designed to encourage group members to get real and be vulnerable. But how your group deals with those vulnerabilities will determine how much deeper your group can go. If a person is sharing something that makes him particularly vulnerable, avoid offering a quick, fix-it answer. Even if you know how to heal deep hurts, cure eating disorders, or overcome depression in one quick answer, hold your tongue. Most people who make themselves vulnerable aren't looking for a quick fix. They want two things: to know they aren't alone and to be supported. If you can identify with their hurt, say so, without one-upping their story with your own. Second, let the person know you'll pray for him, and if the moment is right, go ahead and pray for him right then. If the moment isn't right, then you may want to pray for him at the end of the meeting. Walking through these vulnerable times is tricky business, and it's going to take a lot of prayer and listening to God's leading to get you through.

Some group members don't prepare before our meetings. How can we encourage them to read ahead of time?

It can be frustrating, particularly as a leader, when group members don't read the material; but don't let this discourage you. You can begin each lesson by reading the section together as a group so that everyone is on the same page. And you can gently encourage group members to read during the week. But ultimately, what really matters is that they show up and are growing spiritually alongside you. The REDEFINING LIFE studies aren't about homework; they're about personal spiritual growth, and that takes place in many ways—both inside and outside this book. So if someone's slacking on the outside, it's okay. You have no idea how much she may be growing or being challenged on the inside.

Our group members are having a tough time reaching their goals. What can we do?

First of all, review the goals you've set. Are they realistic? How would you measure a goal of "don't be frustrated at work"? Rewrite the goals until they're bite-sized and reasonable—and reachable. How about "Take an online personality test" or "Make a list of what's good and what's not-so-good about my career choices so I can talk about it with discussion group members" or "Start keeping a prayer journal." Get practical. Get real. And don't forget to marinate everything in lots of prayer.

notes

Lesson 1

1. Stacy Kravetz, *Welcome to the Real World: You've Got an Education—Now Get a Life!* (New York: Norton, 1997), pp. 36-37.
2. Kravetz, pp. 37-38.
3. Rev. Dr. B. Richard Dennis, "The Pin Oak, the Pine, the Pear, and the Pansy," (sermon, January 14, 2001), http://www.pspc.org/sermons/01JAN14.htm.

Lesson 2

1. Dan Miller, *48 Days to the Work You Love* (Nashville: Broadman & Holman, 2005), p. 73.
2. Pamela Rohland, "You've Got Personality: Let It Guide You to the Right Business," *Entrepreneur*, December 2000, http://www.entrepreneur.com/article/0,4621,284048,00.html.
3. "Improve Your Employees' Job Satisfaction," *Technology at Work*, March 22, 2004, http://www.entrepreneur.com/article/0,4621,314871,00.html.

Lesson 3

1. Margaret Feinberg and Leif Oines, *How to Be a Grown-Up: 247 Lab-Tested Strategies for Conquering the World* (Nashville: W Publishing, 2005), pp. 76-79.
2. "Identify Your Glass Ceiling and Attain True Workplace Diversity," *GreaterDiversity.com*, September 28, 2004, http://www.greaterdiversity.com/mt_employer/archives/000053.html.

Lesson 4

1. Bob Rosner, "Working Wounded: Conflict Resolution: Handling Conflicts with Co-Workers," *ABC News*, http://abcnews.go.com/Business/WorkingWounded/story?id=86098&page=1.
2. Michael Warshaw, "The Good Guy's (and Gal's) Guide to Office Politics," *Fast Company*, April 1998, 156.

3. Sharon Salzberg, "Wishing Well," *Oprah.com*, May 2001, http://www
   .oprah.com/relationships/relationships_content.jhtml?contentId=con
   _20020916_wishingwell.xml&section=Friendship&subsection=Celebrate
   +Friendship.

Lesson 5
1. Margaret Feinberg, *What the Heck Am I Going to Do with My Life? Pursue
   Your Passion, Find the Answer* (Chicago: Tyndale, forthcoming).
2. Peter Doskoch, "Are You Your Job?" *Psychology Today*, September/October
   1996, http://cms.psychologytoday.com/articles/pto-19960901-000020
   .html.
3. Matthew Woodley, "Good Pastor, Lousy Leader: How I Came to Terms with
   My Role in the Church," *ChristianityToday.com*, Summer 1999, http://
   www.christianitytoday.com/bcl/areas/leadership/articles/022805.html.
4. Skip Bayless, "Radio Host Prefers Class over Crass," in *More Perfect
   Illustrations for Every Topic and Occasion*, Preaching Today.com, 130
   (Chicago: Tyndale, 2003).

Lesson 6
1. Stress Directions, Inc., "Stress Statistics," *Personal Stress Solutions*, 1999–
   2000, http://www.stressdirections.com/personal/about_stress/stress
   _statistics.html.
2. Thomas H. Holmes and Richard H. Rahe, "The Social Adjustment Rating
   Scale," *Journal of Psychosomatic Research* 11 (1967): 213-218.
3. J. R. Rushik, "Not More Money, More Margin," *Relevant*, n.d., http://www
   .relevantmagazine.com/article.php?sid=613.

Lesson 7
1. Joe Riggio, "My Life as a Fast-Paced Junkie," *Relevant*, n.d., http://www
   .relevantmagazine.com/article.php?sid=6266.
2. Martha Beck, "Balance? Schmalance!" *Oprah.com*, April 2003, http://www
   .oprah.com/omagazine/200304/omag_200304_beck.jhtml.

Lesson 8
1. David Crowder, *Praise Habit: Finding God in Sunsets and Sushi* (Colorado
   Springs, Colo.: NavPress, 2005), pp. 11-14.
2. Richard J. Foster, *Celebration of Discipline: The Path to Spiritual Growth*, 3rd
   ed. (New York: HarperSanFrancisco, 1998), pp. 1-2.

3. Os Hillman, "The Faith at Work Movement: Opening 'The 9 to 5 Window,'" *ChristianityToday.com*, 2004, http://www.christianitytoday .com/workplace/articles/issue9-faithatwork.html.

OWN YOUR FAITH.

Redefining Life: My Purpose

Do you know people who truly believe their life matters? If so, you probably notice that this belief affects everything they do. This raises a deep question for the rest of us: What makes the difference between merely being alive and really living? In this discussion guide, you will be challenged to ask yourself some tough questions about your significance—and where you find it.

TH1NK 1-57683-827-7

Redefining Life: My Identity

So who are you? Only you can know. And part of the journey of self-discovery is God-discovery because He's the One who fashioned you. There is freedom in knowing who you are, and this discussion guide will help with the process. You'll not only discover what you were created for but also learn about the One who created you.

TH1NK 1-57683-828-5

Redefining Life: My Relationships

There are no easy answers when it comes to relationships. But you can develop strong, godly habits to prevent relationship drama before it begins. Learn how you can be a better friend, roommate, boyfriend, or girlfriend with this practical, advice-filled study.

TH1NK 1-57683-888-9

BRINGING TRUTH TO LIFE
www.navpress.com

Visit your local Christian bookstore, call NavPress at 1-800-366-7788, or log on to www.navpress.com to purchase.

To locate a Christian bookstore near you, call 1-800-991-7747.